AF322577

He Found Me

What they did in secret

Brenda Ramos

ISBN: **979-8-9954336-2-0**
LCCN: **2026908397**

This is a nonfiction work. The events are true to the best of the author's memory. The names and identifying details may have been changed to protect the privacy of individuals.

For permissions or inquiries, you may contact the author at hefoundmebr@gmail.com.

Printed in the United States of America

Dedication

To my inner child, the little girl who was neglected and abused. Not only did you survive, you overcame. You did it! You wrote the book, and now your voice is being heard.

To my family, those who became trapped in a box of secrets and were sacrificed in the name of silence.

To all the victims and survivors still fighting to break free, this is my way of uniting my voice with yours so together we become louder.

To my daughters, sons, and all the generations to come. You are the reason I found the courage to break the silence.

Table of Contents

Content Warning

This book contains personal accounts of childhood trauma, including neglect and sexual abuse. Some scenes include graphic and detailed descriptions of abuse and its aftermath. These topics may be triggering for some readers.

Please take care of your emotional well-being as you read. It is okay to take breaks, pause, or skip sections. You are not alone—support, healing, and restoration are possible.

If you or someone you know is in a difficult situation, consider reaching out for help:

United States

National Sexual Assault Hotline

1-800-656-HOPE (4673)

Free, confidential, 24/7

www.RAINN.org

988 Suicide & Crisis Lifeline

Call or text 988

Available 24/7 for emotional distress, suicidal thoughts, or crisis

Closing My Eyes

1

Again, I observed all the oppression that takes place under the sun. I saw the tears of the oppressed, with no one to comfort them. The oppressors have great power, and their victims are helpless.

Ecclesiastes 4:1

I was born on August twenty-seventh, nineteen seventy-nine. Just two days before Hurricane David became a category five hurricane and threatened to pay a visit to the island of Puerto Rico. Like any other newborn, I automatically found a place in my mother's life by becoming her sixth child and her fifth daughter. I'm also the first daughter of her second marriage. It must have been a terrible time to be born, with everyone bracing for a powerful hurricane. Although the storm passed just south of the island, it brought strong winds and heavy rain, flooding, and several deaths in Puerto Rico. When a baby arrives in the middle of chaos, there's usually a story to tell. Everyone must adapt to difficult situations, and that includes me.

It happened when my father wanted some coffee, and I wanted to be fed. We ended up in an unspoken competition, each crying louder to get what we needed. My mom, nervous and overwhelmed, accidentally spilled the hot coffee on herself while trying to manage both of us. The burn left a scar on her body and a mark in my history. That's the story of my birth. I know it by heart. But there must be more to my story; this can't be all there is.

It will be like a woman suffering the pains of labor. When her child is born, her anguish gives way to joy because she has brought a new baby into the world. John 16:21 NLT.

At least that's what I like to think, so I ask my sister to tell me about the story of my birth. I'm waiting for that moment when they finally tell me the part about how happy and excited, they were to meet me. But no one seems to remember those details from my birth.

My mother had five children from her first marriage: Emilia, the oldest, followed by Aida, Mara, William, and Tanairi. One day, their father came home early from work and found our mother with my father. Shortly after, she divorced him and married my father. Emilia is the one who tells me this story the most. She never forgets to add, "Because you were born, my parents couldn't get back together."

My father was an alcoholic. And just like my mother chose him over her first husband, my father chose alcohol over his now family. They got divorced when I was two years old. In that case I can't blame my sisters for holding a grudge against my father. They became the sacrifice in a love affair that didn't last. Each person in my family seems to hold a small piece of the beginning of my story, each one with their perspective and truth. But the one thing I've felt clearly over the years is their resentment. So far, no one has said anything kind about my arrival. On the contrary, I became an inconvenience.

Being a divorced woman with children has always been a challenging endeavor. It is difficult to take on the role of both mother and father, especially without support. My mother searched for ways to rise above the obstacles and silence the many critics. One step she took toward a better life was surrendering her heart to Jesus. Hoping to find peace, she became a Christian, and to appease God, or so she thought, she agreed to follow a long list of rules. One of them was to change the way she dressed. She stopped wearing pants, makeup, and jewelry. But even after all that, life didn't get easier. Trials kept pushing her to the edge. While searching for the love of God, she ended up buried under the laws of men.

Longing for God's acceptance, she was judged by the religious people. For her, religion became another set of chains rather than the peace and freedom she had hoped to find.

We were living in Dorado, Puerto Rico. It was a hot and sunny day when Mom took all six of us to the beach. We played in the water, enjoyed the breeze, and built sandcastles together. It felt like a happy moment to spend quality time as a family. Then suddenly, right there on the sand, a group of guys from church crossed our path. They looked at my mother and began shouting at her, calling us out, "You're going to hell, sons of the devil!" All because she was wearing shorts. Not a swimsuit or something outrageous, but shorts and not the "Christian uniform." Which was a blouse and a long skirt.

As they cursed and humiliated us, one of the men stomped on our sandcastle. What had taken time, effort, and joy to build was destroyed within seconds. In that moment, it felt like our family was fragile and made of porcelain. As a vase that had been dropped, we shattered. That sandcastle became a living symbol of our home: something good we tried to build, only to have it crushed by the feet of someone claiming to represent God. That day, my mom stopped going to church, and religion became a scar in my family. The adversary then took a chance and strengthened the spiritual bonds.

I don't have any memories from this day. But it is one of those stories that Aida tells me every time she is having a rough day. She believes God punishes people when they turn away from him. Therefore, God is punishing us.

I feel like something in me is changing. I've been sleeping, and now it's time for me to wake up. Can I get a few more minutes? Just a little longer before I open my eyes to start living with a conscience. I'm not ready to be awakened. It is too early; I'm not ready yet.

As I opened my eyes, I put on my new clothes: a red polo shirt with a navy-blue pleated skirt. This will be my uniform. For the first time, I'll be attending school. I get excited, skipping around the house, happy and full of energy. Then I hear her shouting, Take off your uniform and go to your room. I'd rather not see you! Oh no, that's my mother shouting. She must be mad. I better run and hide from her. I need to close my eyes; it's not safe.

Mom, look! I know how to tie my shoes. Wait, I already tied them earlier. Mom, could you show me how to tie my shoes? Go and ask one of your sisters. I'm not your teacher, she replied. I feel sad. I just wanted her to be proud of me. I'm sure Tanairi will teach me, and she does. I try again and show my mom, but she doesn't even look at me. Her face is blank, with no expression at all. I feel disappointed. This is not the reaction I was hoping for. But it's okay; she's always too busy to pay attention to me.

Mom, can you give me a hug? I ask her in a quiet, careful voice. As I walk toward her, she pushes me away. Stop being so clingy and grow up; you're five years old, she says. I can't hold back my tears. I run upstairs and lock myself in the bedroom before she gets mad.

Aida, why doesn't Mom love me? I ask through tears. That's how Mom is. Stop giving her hugs and kisses, she replies.

In school, we were working on a family project. I had to fill in the blanks on the questions about my family. What are the names of my parents? Where do they work? Who lives in my home?

Do I have a father? I asked innocently. Yes, Brenda, my teacher replied, "all the kids have one". I felt ashamed for asking aloud.

At home, I said, Mom, the teacher wants to know who my father is. She said every kid has one, so I must too. I had been asking all day, and she kept avoiding me. Until she got annoyed and answered my questions. I was supposed to fill in the blanks and find out who I am. Instead, I felt belittled and rejected by my mom's answers.

Brenda, you were born by a coincidence, a mistake. That is all you are. Tell your teacher that your father is nobody. An alcoholic. His name is "Drunk. "There, that's all about your father, she answered. So here I am, back in school, getting yelled at by my teacher because I told the whole class that my father's name was Drunk.

This created some sort of curiosity in me. Do I have a father? Maybe my mom is lying about who my dad is. Why did she leave her husband for him if he is not good enough?

Months passed, and I kept trying to capture glimpses of life that I could understand. Little things I learned at school and noticed at home. Most of my days just seemed to disappear as the day went by. If I closed my eyes, I wouldn't know what was going on around me, and I wouldn't feel anything either. When my eyes are open, I record everything. With every detail being stored inside my memory.

Every so often, Emilia comes home to visit with her husband and kids. My mom likes him because he works and has a car. He would take us to his house in Dorado, Puerto Rico. There was a small window with a view of the ocean. I could see the waves coming and going, crashing into the shore, as if dancing to a song. Eddy stood behind me so close that I could hear him breathing. I would rather not record that. I focused on the waves instead. I stared at them hard, as if I could make them speak louder than anything else. At first, they looked peaceful, but then they became angry and agitated. Crashing violently into the shore, only to retreat in fear. Just like them, I retreated and closed my eyes.

We usually go to the beach and spend the day there. Sometimes, though, Mom will go to a different spot to fish with Eddy and his friends. For some reason, I always follow her. Maybe I am just being the baby of the house. Mom stops in the middle of the woods and does bad things with Eddy's friends. I turn around and look the other way, pretending not to hear or see. But I just know it's bad. They drink alcohol and laugh at my mother's effort to entertain them. While I just sit quietly on a rock, staring at the water. Sinking within my emotions, waiting for someone to fish me out of this family.

When Emilia visits us in Cataño, Puerto Rico, I hide from Eddy. I don't like it when he finds me and touches my private parts. He laughs like it's some type of game: ready or not, here I come! Pretend that he didn't see me and then shout, I found you! He knows how Mom likes to punish us with her silence. She will never listen to us and will always choose any men before us. He knew my family, our secrets, and our mischievousness. He also knew my hiding spots and would always find me. Except when I am quick to hide under a bed. Then he can't touch me. Here under the bed, I am safe.

Aida has a boyfriend. He's been visiting her for a few weeks now. Oh, here he comes again. I ran up to the room and told Aida that her boyfriend had arrived. She doesn't say anything. She just stays quiet and then starts to cry. It turns out Pin isn't here to see Aida; he's here to see Mom. Now Pin is dating my mother.

He comes over almost every night. They drink alcohol and listen to bolero. That's the kind of music older people listen to. Bolero music means that the night will be long, and Mom will have a friend over. We know the rules. Don't go downstairs to interrupt her because you will be punished. We stayed hidden upstairs, quiet in our bedrooms. If Mom hears us, if she even hears us breathing, she'll come up and beat us all one by one. It is difficult to fall asleep with loud music, but after a while you get used to it.

I'm asleep, but I feel uncomfortable; there's something wrong with my body. I open my eyes, and there is Pin sitting on my bed. He is touching my private parts. Shh… don't you dare make noise! This became his nightly routine, waking me up with his aggressive touch. When he comes over, I try to stay awake. He doesn't make any noise when he comes up the stairs and walks the hall, but I still can feel his presence getting close. What if I sleep on the opposite side of the bed? Then, instead of him touching my lips with his private part, he will touch my feet. I'm exhausted from lack of sleep.

— Mom, last night, Pin came into my room. He comes to my room, and he… My mother interrupted me with a slap on the face and said, you are a liar; go to your room! I ran to my room and threw myself on the bed. I don't understand why she slapped me; how can she say I'm a liar if she didn't even hear what I had to say? He touched me. He touched me, I whispered while I cried myself to sleep.

To be punished by Mom means that she will stop talking to you for days or even weeks. She doesn't look at me or acknowledge that I'm alive. The strange thing is that her silence also brings relief. Pin is also ignoring me. He still goes upstairs to the second floor, but now he goes into my sister Mara's room. I think he's touching her too. But unlike me, she seems to like it; she kisses him and touches him in return. Mara is Pin's new girlfriend.

Mom called me and said so casually with a smile, like it was nothing. You were right. Pin goes up to the rooms. So, I dared to ask, Mom, can you say you're sorry? She asked, who do you think you are? I'm your mother! I will never apologize to you. Go to your room until you learn how to stay quiet. With her actions, I understood that she wasn't concerned about the fact that Pin was going up to the rooms or that he touched me. She was just mad that he was dating Mara. For me, the whole thing became something to be ashamed of. But I learned that this is a part of my family tradition. One man can date my mom and her daughters. Like we were a recycling company.

Soon after, my mom started a relationship with a married man. One night, she got him drunk, and he fell asleep on the sofa. When he did, she took pictures of him with an instant camera. She gave me the photo, and I used it as a fan until the picture appeared on the photo paper. She didn't know how to take pictures. He was lying with his eyes closed, with no shirt, on an ugly yellow sofa. However, my mom found it amusing, as she was unable to hold back her laughter.

A few weeks later, she took me to this fancier neighborhood. There, she gave me an envelope with pictures, including the photo of him sleeping. I was given the instructions to knock on a specific door.

I knocked on the door and gave the envelope away to his wife. As she opened it and looked at the pictures, I saw the look of sadness and pain in her eyes. I felt like I understood her. That's how I feel when my mom does things to belittle me. Without a word, she can break my heart into tiny pieces. That was the look of a heartbreak.

Aida started a new relationship with Manny, who lived just down the street from us. One evening Mom beat her up in public. I remember watching as my mom dragged Aida by the hair, pulling her all the way down the street and into our house. That day, Aida had had enough. She packed her things and moved out with Manny and his parents.

Not long after that, Emilia divorced Eddy and moved with her two kids into an apartment right around the corner from us. Almost immediately, she met a man named Oswaldo, and he moved in with her. But Oswaldo was cruel. He didn't like my nephew just because he was a boy. To please him, Emilia sent her son to live with Eddy. Like a toy, she gave him up and decided to stay with only the girl. Oswaldo didn't like any males at all. Not even animals. He had a male dog, and he would beat him too. He seemed to get along with females, especially with my sister Mara, who had broken up with Pin and was now single. I try not to record too much of what happens in my family. The dynamic is confusing, scary, and full of secrets that are too heavy to carry. So, I do what I've always done. I hide within myself, and I close my eyes when it's not safe.

We are all girls, except for my brother. So, there's always a boyfriend around who gets treated like a king. This is how my family works.

It is time to grow up; now I am no longer the youngest in the house.

My mother had a new daughter. I have a little sister named Leilani. She is beautiful with light skin and green eyes. I promise myself to take care of her. Leilani, like the rest of us, doesn't have a father. The teacher says we all have one, but none of our fathers are present. They've all abandoned us, and I wonder if I even have a mother.

One day at school, two older boys took me to the backyard. It was an isolated place, with nothing but very tall grass. Suddenly, my brother William appeared and asked me to leave. As usual, I did as I was told and walked away. I put distance between myself and the boys. I hadn't gone that far when I heard my brother's voice. I looked back and saw them holding him against the wall. Instantly, a wave of anger rose inside me. You're a boy; why don't you defend yourself? I whispered with a low and trembling voice. Just like my sisters, I turned my back on him and kept walking. But I didn't make it far. I stumbled over a rock and fell onto the grass. In moments like these, gravity feels heavier, almost like it's trying to keep me down. While lying there, I noticed wildflowers hiding quietly among the grass. They looked so fragile that I was glad I hadn't stumbled on them. Tears ran down my cheeks as I whispered, do not worry, little flowers. I won't tell anyone you're hiding here. It's our secret. No one will step on you. Then the bell rang. It was time to return to class. I stood up and walked back to my classroom like any other day, as if I was only coming back from lunch.

When the school day ended, I went back home. What had I done? My mom looked at me like she wanted to kill me, and my brother's glare felt like a death sentence. I'm used to it. Without saying a word, I went straight to hide in my room.

My brother did not go back to school after that day. I never really understood why he dropped out. But every time they talk about school, they blame me, saying it is my fault. I wish I knew what he meant by it was because of me. But I do know this much: it's not my fault. I never asked him to save me and take my place.

My mom went out and left us home alone for a few days. She tends to do this because she says that she needs a break from us. Leilani has been crying nonstop. There's no milk for her to be fed. Tanairi is my mom's personal babysitter. Mara still lives with us, but she never comes out of her room. So, it's my job to go out and either find our mom or find milk. But I don't know where to go. I look for her at the bar and at that apartment where people go to do drugs. I'm running around in circles, hoping to catch a glimpse of her. Going back and forth empty-handed, feeling lost and small.

I stop by Aida's house, but Mom isn't there either. Aida, I ask, can I please have a little milk to take home for Leilani? She says no. My heart sinks, but I start heading back home. Aida is still living with Manny's family, and her bedroom is the last one down the hall on the second floor. Just before I reach the steps, her father-in-law calls out to me. He tells me to come into the room. I pause. I know it's inappropriate to go into people's bedrooms. But perhaps he can help. Once I stepped inside his bedroom, he asked me to get closer. He was lying down on the bed. Do you know where my mom is? I asked. Without saying a word to me, he reached for my arm and pulled me toward him. Then he touched me in between my legs. I couldn't move. I was paralyzed while he was smiling and enjoying the moment. Does he think I like being touched?

I felt glued to the floor; my legs didn't work anymore. My eyes searched the room for a way to escape, but instead they landed on a painting hanging on the wall. The painter did a bad job. I couldn't tell what it was supposed to be. A mess of colors blurred and unfinished. A mess of emotions that was unable to form a picture, just like me.

Brenda, you can go. I hear Aida's voice calling my name. She sounded far away. Slowly I looked at her, and there she was, standing next to me. Her father-in-law was gone. "He's done. Go home," she said, laughing. I didn't understand what was funny. As soon as I felt my legs again, I fled, running without stopping all the way home.

A few hours later, my mom came home. I waited for the right moment, then quietly said to her, Mom… Ñin touched me. At first, she just giggled. Then she asked me, If you know he's a dirty old man, why did you get close to him? Everyone knows he can't keep his hands to himself. That's what you get for getting close to him.

I stayed silent; I didn't know the answer to her question. Replaying in my mind the moment I got close to him. I needed to find her. I couldn't reply, so I ran to my room, and there I cried myself to sleep.

Still Waiting

2

My soul, wait in silence for God alone,
for my hope is from Him.

Psalm 62:5 NASB

All along, I knew who my father was, but he was nothing like my "dream father." I still held in my heart the hope of meeting him one day. The father I created in my mind was perfect. He loved me, acknowledged me, and truly cared. A protector, strong like a superhero, always ready to fight against evil.

I have to be responsible and go out to look for my mother. We'd been left home alone, and my brother is on the verge of an episode. I tried to calm him, but nothing lasted. I knew where she might be, probably at a bar nearby. And yes, I found her. Just as I expected, she was drunk, barely able to stand straight. Therefore, when she agreed to come home with me, I felt like I'd won a war without having to fight. I guess today is my lucky day.

When Mom drinks, she believes she's the sexiest woman alive and acts like every other woman is beneath her. She's convinced she can get any man's attention, even if it means getting naked in public. We were just around the corner from home when a man called out to her. He was sitting on a chair, drinking a beer. Without hesitation, my mother walked over and sat on his lap. I was surprised because when she's sober, she can't stand him. He's a public bus driver. The kind who never lets her ride unless she has the money upfront. Here she is, sitting on his lap, kissing him. I felt embarrassed.

The man reached out and grabbed my hand, pulling me closer to them. I was standing so close, he reached out and touched my breast. Then he slid his hand between my legs and touched my private part. Shame burned through me. It feels like everyone is watching from across the street; everyone could see exactly what was happening. Since there were people drinking outside the bar, across the street.

No. I don't want him to touch me. I pushed his hand away from between my legs. But he grabbed me; he tried again, and I pushed him one more time. That's when he grabbed my hand tightly, holding it in place. My mother was still on his lap, still kissing him. He was kissing her and staring at me. Across the street, my father was sitting at the bar. From there he could see everything. But the only thing he cares about is his Palo Viejo rum bottle.

Tears come running down my cheeks, like a torrential downpour falling from the sky with no warning. Each teardrop hits with force, leaving me gasping for air. I'm scared. What if people think I like these bad things? What if they believe I want this? I can't close my eyes. His hand is still squeezing mine so tightly, it hurts.

Finally, my mother stands up and decides it's time to go home. We take only a few steps before she turns on me. She pushes me, and I fall. Each time I get up from the ground, she pushes me again. Then she slaps me across the face. You always ruin my peace! She tells me with an angry tone. I can't be happy because of you; you are always getting in my way. It's always you!

I must be the worst daughter in the world if I'm able to ruin my mother's happiness. I'm a burden, and it's my fault she's unhappy.

It is because of me that my brother has schizophrenia; he got sick when he saved me that day in school. I must be a mistake, a worthless girl who ruins people's lives. And that thought makes me sad, because I've been trying for the last two years to make my mother happy, and I failed; I can't please her.

I'm almost eight years old, and I still can't get her to love me. I haven't earned it. Maybe if I ask her for forgiveness, things will be better. But first, I have to stop crying. I need to hide under the bed. If she hears me, she'll get mad, and she'll hit me again.

Mom, can you forgive me for ruining your life? I asked. She didn't hesitate. No, Brenda. I can't forgive you. The only one who can is God. But He won't forgive you either. She looked me in the eyes and continued saying, That's why you're here on earth. He sent you as a punishment. You misbehaved in heaven, and He kicked you out.

I ran to my room, and there I asked Tanairi, Who is God? She paused for a moment, then answered, God? He's just like us. He doesn't have a father or a mother. She leaned in a little to whisper, You can't ask too many questions about Him. Just forget about him. You'll never see Him anyway because if you do, you'll die. She looked away and said, God is just God. The one to create Adam and Eve and the one that punishes us when we do something bad.

Last night I couldn't sleep thinking about God until I figured out the mystery of where He is. Now, I can't wait to get out of school so I can run to the front yard and talk to Him. Maybe I'll have a point in my favor. I'm sure He'll give me a chance once He hears me. I'm glad today is Friday. Weekends are meant to be spent with family. The kids at school tell stories about their weekend adventures. For the first time, just like them, I'll be going on a journey. A magical journey back home. I'm not afraid. I know I won't perish when I talk to God. I'll keep my head down to avoid eye contact with him. I believe with all my heart that God will come for me. He will forgive me.

God, I know you're hiding in the sun. That's why no one can see you, and if they do, they die. I don't mind if you kill me. I just want you to know that I'm sorry. Please, God, forgive me. I promise, if you take me back to heaven, I'll behave. I know you sent me to Earth to punish me. God, did I touch the angels in their private parts? I'm sorry. I understand why you didn't want me in heaven. You were right to kick me out. I deserved it. You wanted me to feel what it's like when someone touches you; it hurts. God, if you threw me out of heaven for doing bad things… where do you send people who touch others on Earth? Do you throw them from planet to planet?

God, I've learned my lesson. I won't do it ever again. You're so far away, I'm not even sure you can hear me. Still… I'll be here, waiting. Your hiding place is safe with me. I won't tell anyone about the sun. I don't want you to get sick like I do when I have to find a new hiding spot. I'll keep your secret safe. I thought God was coming to pick me up. I sat outside under the sun, but he didn't show. Still, every day I wait for Him. There's a Bible in my bedroom, always open to Psalm 91. Mom says we're not allowed to read it. People who read the Bible go crazy because they ask questions, and there are no answers. I stay away from it. Well, sometimes I get curious and read a few lines while I pretend to clean around it.

Sometimes people from church come to the plaza to preach. When they do, my mother turns off all the lights and shuts the doors and windows to pretend no one is home. There's always a group going door-to-door, inviting people. Today, I sat on the floor near the window so I could hear them. They must know God, right?

Stupid me! The preacher only talked about sin and how people were going straight to hell. Stupid preacher, I'm already in hell.

If he knows God so well, why doesn't he tell people how to get to heaven? He must not know Him at all. He seems to know more about hell than heaven, and he screamed so much he gave me a headache. I'm going to lie down. My head is pounding, and I'm disappointed.

I've been trying not to cry myself to sleep. It makes my nose stuffy, and I can't breathe quietly. That's why I've started wetting the bed at night. I cry in my sleep, and my body is trying to let the tears out another way. I think there are too many tears inside me. I even put a cup under my bed to collect them, but then I forget to do so every time I cry. When it rains, I think God is crying. The clouds can't hold His tears, just like my eyes can't hold mine. Perhaps God feels sad because I touched some angels, and they are in pain just like me.

Aida moved into an apartment, and every time I visit, her husband plays porn movies on the TV. That's what a woman needs to do, he says, or she's useless. I feel disgusted for being a female. There are times when Manny makes me lie down on their bed. He says he can hypnotize me. He has a necklace, a special one with powers. When he uses it, you will do what he says. That's what it means to be hypnotized. You can't resist it, or else the hypnosis won't work. If it doesn't work, he says, you could stay hypnotized forever, which means you'll go crazy for the rest of your life. If you obey, everything will go back to normal. You won't remember anything. That's why you need to lie down for safety. I wonder what kind of silly stuff I've done. He never tells me. I can't ask Aida because she always leaves the room. I don't like it when he hypnotizes me, but I'm too scared to say no. He says if I refuse, the necklace will haunt me in my dreams.

My mother's parents and sister came from the United States to visit, and they're staying with us. I don't like that I'm expected to give them a hug and a kiss and to act excited just because they're here. I've become just like my mom; I don't like giving hugs and kisses.

Today we're supposed to go to the beach. I already have my swimsuit on, and I'm just sitting here on the balcony, waiting. Then my dad shows up. He opens the gate and carries me away from home. As we get further, sadness creeps in. I was really looking forward to going to the beach. Since we never go out as a family. Suddenly, I'm almost back at the house. Everything is a blur. My mom is pushing me away, and I'm crying. My mom and her sister are yelling. They're beating my dad. Her sister has a baseball bat, and she's hitting him. He falls to the ground, and there's blood running from his head. Even her father is hitting him with his cane. Why are they doing this? What did he do wrong? I try to help him, but my mom strikes me and tells me to go. No one helps. People are watching. More and more people gather, but no one steps in.

I can't breathe. My head hurts, and my heart is beating fast. Home is a few steps away, but it feels too far. I can see Tanairí on the porch. She's calling to me with her arms reaching, waving me home. Somehow, I made it. She grabs my hand and pulls me inside, closing the gate behind us. I run to my bedroom, close my windows, and hide under my bed. Covering my ears with my hands. My heart is still trying to break through my chest. Stop recording. Close your eyes!

The old lady couldn't have kids; along with my mother's uncle, she raised my mother and two other girls as their own. They're not my real grandparents. I shouldn't have to love them. I don't need to; we're not even blood related. I'm not the one who ruined my mother's life; they did. It's not my fault; it's theirs.

I've been lying on the yellow sofa all day. I feel sick and have a fever. I want to go to my room, but I keep falling asleep here in the living room. I woke up because there's a lot of commotion. The old lady swears she bought some bananas, and someone stole them. Mom tells her to check her room because she probably hid them herself. Who would even want to steal bananas? Still, everyone is looking.

Lydia, my mom's sister, is pretending to help. She asks me if I know where the bananas are, as if I'm the one hiding them. She sits next to me and puts her hands under my blanket. Are you sure you're not hiding them? She laughs at me and pulls down my pants and underwear. Be quiet and be still. I'm going to make sure you're not hiding them. She says while she puts her hand between my legs and her fingers inside me.

My mom is in the kitchen. I can see her from where I am. My eyes are wide open, but as usual, no sound comes out. No matter how badly I want to scream, I just can't. Then Mom walks toward the living room. We look at each other. We're locked in a stare, like some kind of contest. And then… she turns around and walks away. I stayed there, eyes glued to her, following her with my stare. Lydia is smoking now that she's tired of touching me. She says, oh, you are dirty. You need to be cleansed. As she proceeds to burn me between my legs with her lit cigarette. Even then, I stay silent.

All this time, I thought my mom didn't see what was going on right in front of her eyes. Maybe she was like me. Perhaps she had her eyes closed. But now I know she's nothing like me, and I'm nothing like her. I close my eyes because I'd rather not record so many bad moments in my memory. I might look like a robot on the outside, but inside, I'm hiding a real girl. A girl I would rather not get ruined. Mom turns away on purpose. She doesn't want any of us to surpass her. She wants to prove that I am worthless and my life means nothing. My mother is not my mom; she's a stranger, and I hate her.

I want to die. I wish I could die. But even when I feel desperate, I must be quiet. So, I just write in my school notebook, over and over again, "I want to die." I also wrote a letter to myself, so I won't forget to write a book about all the things they do to me when I'm older. Since my mom wants me to be quiet, I will do the opposite. If I don't die, I will write a book. Luckily, my mother found the notebook and punished me. She said she will keep the notebook as proof that I am crazy and suicidal.

I feel that my brother takes advantage of his condition. He screams and slams doors, while my sisters and I hide in fear. When he sees me playing and laughing, he tells his mom that I'm mocking him. If I'm serious, he says I'm staring at him meanly. Every time, Mom asks me to apologize and make him happy because, after all, it's my fault.

I came to school early and stayed waiting in front of my classroom for the bell to ring. The kids are playing; I could join them if I wanted to, run around, and be free. Instead, I'd rather save my energy; I know it's going to be a long day.

My brother was rocking himself violently in the rocking chair, with his right hand on his forehead like he was thinking while talking in another language. I say it's another language because no one can understand him. He talks to himself, and that's how his tantrum begins. I know he's my brother, and I'm supposed to understand him because he's sick. But I am being held accountable for his constant outbursts. I would rather be touched every single day of my life than repay him for his so-called good deed. I didn't ask him to save me. I could have handled the situation. I didn't need him; he's the one who needs me to be happy. I already paid a high price, and it's a secret.

From the second floor at school, I can see my house. My brother is still rocking, and his mom is walking from the kitchen to him. She gives him something to drink, probably juice with his medications. I hate them both. They disgust me. It's a new feeling; I am blinded by anger. Yesterday, I spent all day writing in my notebook that I wanted to die. And now I'm here at school, and I don't need to breathe quietly. I hate you! I scream with all the strength in me. I hate you! I hate you, and I hate your mom. As usual, she didn't hear me. I screamed it so loud, I don't think I have any sound left in me. There is complete silence in the whole school.

I'm tired. I can't wait any longer for God to end his punishment. I can't continue living like this. I want to die. I climbed the rails and let go of myself. One of the parents grabbed me when I let go and carried me to the nurse's office. From there, I was taken to the hospital. I kept opening and closing my eyes enough to take a few pictures. I felt like the camera in my mind was crashing, frozen in the middle of two lives. I'm caught between being a living rag doll and a little girl who is trapped in a cage. Still waiting to be rescued.

Businessmen

3

They cast lots for my people
and traded boys for prostitutes;
they sold girls for wine to drink.

Joel 3:3 NLT.

I'm being raised only by a mother figure. My brother is the only male, but he is not taking the role of a man. My mother doesn't work, so she's very limited with finances, and so is our food supply. I inherit my clothes from my older sisters. I have to take good care of them because I'll pass them on to my baby sister. I'm constantly sent to the store with a note asking for food, promising my mom will repay them later, kind of like a credit. Many times, they say no. Other times, the men take me to the storage room, and if I behave, then they give me food to take home.

When she cooks, my brother has to be served before anyone else. He also gets a bigger portion and doesn't have to share his drinks or sweets. From a pack of six cookies, we each get one, while he eats the whole thing. He gets to drink juice or soda, and we get one sip each or plain water. Some days, he throws the food across the kitchen before we can even eat. His tantrums are more frequent now that I'm no longer his personal entertainer. Almost every episode guarantees a punishment for me. I end up hiding under my bed, and we all end up starving. My mother says she needs a break from this house, so she leaves us alone for days at a time. When she's gone, Tanairí takes care of us, and I take care of my brother. I wish I could disappear for a few days... or forever. I require a break too.

My belly always hurts because I'm hungry. I get tired of drinking water and eating ice cubes. So, I found a way to feed myself. There are so many trees and plants in the yard; no one will ever notice I'm eating the leaves. My sister also makes chocolate cake or soup with soil and rocks. The rocks are like potatoes, but we can't eat them; they're too hard. She makes coffee with dirt and water, but I don't drink coffee. I'm a child. I always pretend it's chocolate milk.

Since the day I had a mental breakdown in school, I haven't been back. But unlike my brother, I don't get a free pass. I'm expected to go out to the stores and pharmacy to get his medication. My mother always says, 'If you're not going to calm him down, then you must go to the pharmacy while I make sure, he doesn't kill your sisters." I gladly run the errands. It gives me a chance to breathe pure air, since the one at home is poisoned by their presence. Every time I'm around them for too long, the air makes me sick. I can't breathe.

Not every man is bad to me. When my mom sends me to the gambling house, they are nice. One of them always says, little girl, you again! I laugh and hand him the list with the numbers she wants to play. There are always guns and money on the tables. Sometimes I sit on the ground, just watching. I would like to learn from them, but they always kick me out, saying, this is no place for a little girl. I don't think he knows my name, and I don't know his. One day, he asked, "When is your mom going to learn not to send you? He didn't like seeing me there. What if the police come? I offered to be on the lookout in exchange for food. He just smiled and said no.

After that day, he started giving me food for free. I asked him if he wanted me to watch out for the police. He said no. I asked if he wanted to touch me or kiss me like the rest, and he said no. The man with the bad reputation is the only one who was good to me. Whenever I ran into him while playing the lottery or placing bets on horse races for my mom, he'd ask me to pick a horse. He'd give me money because he knew my horse was going to win. He asked me to buy food just for me and to hide it. 'It's yours alone," he'd say. Of course, I shared it with my sisters and hid it from my mother and brother. How I wish that man would have been my father.

My mom gave me a list to take to my father. She asked me not to come back until I got everything. I know she's mad at me. Her son is about to have a tantrum, and when she asked me to calm him down, I said no. I can see in her eyes that she wants to slap me, but she also needs me to get the food. She hopes for him to feel special by preparing his favorite dish. As always, I would rather run errands. It's not that difficult to find my dad; he's usually drunk, sitting in the same corner. Before I left, I dressed up in a short blue skirt, and I felt pretty. I want my brother to see me happy. He hates it when I smile, especially when he's about to have an episode. I'm not afraid of him!

My dad was drunk, sitting in the same place—he was easy to find. "Hi Dad, my mom sent you this list." I can feel his anger as he snapped, "You're just like your mom; you only come up to me when you require something. And just like her, you look like a slut in that skirt. Are you wearing shorts? You better are, or I'll slap you."

"Dad, the skirt has shorts attached. I'm not like my mother." As I spoke, he reached out and put his hand under my skirt to check if I was wearing shorts. But my dad didn't take his hand from under my skirt; he is now touching me. He stared at me with his irritated red eyes. See, he said, you're just like your mom; you like it. He grabs my face roughly with his other hand and kisses me on the mouth. His alcoholic, foul breath tasted as strong as horse manure. Once again, I was paralyzed. After what felt like an eternity, he stood up and walked away. Then he came back with two paper bags with food for my mom. "This is how you do business with a whore," he said.

I brought home food, just as my mother demanded. Am I now the man of the house? At what cost do I supply food?

Dinner was served! Mom would whistle from the bottom of the stairs and leave our plates on the floor. I ran down and kept going to the front yard. I didn't pick up my plate. There was a bush with some green, round fruits. People say they are poisonous, but that was my dinner. It gave me a bad tummy ache. My body cramped in pain, and so did my soul. I was hurting so much that I lay down on my bed and waited for death. After all, that's all I wanted: to die.

The morning after I arrived, and here I am, alive. There's this awful pain inside me. It's not in my tummy or my heart, but somewhere deep in between. I probably slept in because I can hear them talk from the living room. Of course, it's only my mother and brother. The rest of us can't make any noise. They sound happy. I can understand my brother; he's not talking in this weird language. I'm pretty sure he is relaxed; after all, he is the man of the house, and he doesn't have to go out and get food. He's not the provider I am. Mom doesn't have to go out and do business. Why would she when she has me? When she was sober, she would jump the fence in the backyard instead of walking out through the gate. She hides from people. While I have to go out, get exposed and fulfill her demands.

I can't take this anymore! Where is God? Why doesn't He forgive me? It hurts, an invisible pain that's killing me slowly. It hurts to be the one who ruins everyone's life. To feel that my worth is just a bag of food, medicine, and loans. It's a curse to be guilty. To be the exchange in the hands of the businessmen. I'm paralyzed in my thoughts. There's a heavy weight pressing down on my chest, making it impossible to stay afloat. I'm sinking deeper into my bed. My life feels like a trap. I'm sick just like my brother is sick.

With every ounce of strength I have, I scream, loud and desperate, over and over again until I black out. Starting all over as I regain consciousness. My mom takes me to the hospital. I wish to disappear. I don't want to be here. Why can't anyone understand? I want to close my eyes and become the little girl hiding away. The pure, innocent girl that no one can touch. Inside me, two girls are at war: one is broken and wants to die, and the other is pure and wants to survive. I can't stop screaming. I pass out repeatedly, capturing only blurry glimpses.

From the local hospital, they transfer me by ambulance to a better-equipped place. The doctors try to keep me awake, holding a small cloth near my face. I see their lips moving, but their words are lost in silence. Staying awake is hard, and honestly, I don't want to be. I lie there, hooked to an IV in my arm and wires on my chest, finally breathing clean air through an oxygen mask. The doctors speak, but I can't hear them. A young doctor shines a flashlight in my eyes and shakes me every time I start to drift off, asking me, What's your name? I stare back silently; for once, my mind is quiet too. Even if I wanted to answer, I don't know who I am. I'm losing myself, and it's because of my mom and brother. They are driving me crazy.

I was admitted to the hospital for a few days. There's nothing medically wrong physically. Therefore, I was treated as a mental health patient. Like my brother, I now have an appointment with a psychiatrist. Therefore, my mom is angry and doesn't want to take me. You think I have time for you? She keeps asking. You always have to make things worse. I don't have time for you.

On the way to my first appointment, she doesn't say a word. Only when we sit in the waiting room does she speak: Psychiatrists always end up going crazy because they deal with so many people's problems. I don't want you to talk too much. If you stay quiet, maybe you'll be able to go home. You don't want to stay in the hospital with crazy people, do you?

The psychiatrist calls me in, and I go alone. His office is small, and his desk is huge. There isn't even enough room to breathe. He keeps asking me questions, but I don't know how to answer. When he asks, what do you like? I reply, I like it when there's silence. When I was in the hospital, I couldn't hear a thing. No loud TV, no shouting or slamming doors, and no bolero music at night. My mind felt quiet and empty. I loved it. I love it when there's silence.

Then he asks, what don't you like? I say, I don't like it when people say bad words like 'stupid' or 'whore.' I don't like my family or keeping secrets. What secrets are you keeping? He asks. I can't tell you; it's a secret. I don't want to talk anymore; you are making me sick. I feel like I can't breathe. Stop asking, stop!

He agrees: Okay, let's not talk anymore. Let's draw a picture of your family so I can meet them. He passes me a paper and crayons across his desk. I then draw my sisters and me inside little squares because we hide in our rooms. Next to each square is a black shadow waiting. My mom and brother stand outside the squares because they can be anywhere in the house. My brother is a stick figure because he is weak, and I give him an extra line in his private part because he is different from mine. I'm proud of my drawing. It's picture-perfect.

My mother is mad at me because I talk too much. She said she's not taking me back to the psychiatrist because he is now crazy. What happens in the house stays in the house, she said. I felt sorry for the psychiatrist. He listened to me, and now his life is ruined.

Days passed, and Eddy stopped by to visit. Today doesn't feel like a good day. I can sense something is wrong. I have a dog named Susie, who is white with black spots. I barely spend time with her because I'm constantly trying to stay one step ahead of my brother. The real girl in me only comes out when it's safe, and Susie makes her happy. She lets you hug her, and she gives you kisses by licking your face. Susie is not like Mom; she can genuinely love you.

My sister said goodbye to Susie, but I didn't understand why; Susie never leaves the house. Tanairí told me to say goodbye. I asked, why? She said Eddy was taking Susie because Mom didn't want her anymore. I asked Mom if it was true, but she just asked me to shut up. I asked Eddy and he said, yes, I'm putting her in a trash bag in the trunk of my car and dumping her in the water for her to drown. Tears ran down my face like a waterfall, and I begged them not to do it. Mom pushed me away while Eddy just laughed.

Why? I asked. Because she's a girl, and I'm tired of her, Mom answered. She gets her period, and all the dogs are after her. I'm sick and tired of raising so many bitches in this house. I kept crying, begging her not to kill Susie. Can we give her away to someone as a present? I pleaded. Please don't kill her! But Mom told me to be quiet, or she will do the same to me. I stayed silent as Eddy took Susie away in the trash bag. I didn't have an opportunity to say goodbye to her. I feel like Susie got killed as a punishment for me. I feel guilty.

Today I'm on a field trip to the pool with the kids from the neighborhood. Once we got there, the kids were jumping in the pool and having fun. I can't do the same because I don't know how to swim. So, I'm just sitting on the edge, quietly splashing my feet.

At home, Tanairí tried to die by swallowing some pills. I told my mom, and she beat her up. Now, Tanairí is mad at me. She asked me why I didn't let her die in peace. I just don't think pills work. They don't work for my brother; I'm the one who calms him down. They also don't work for Aida when she wants to sleep forever. Besides, sometimes I pay a high price to get medicine. Why waste them?

I want to die too, but I don't know how. I'm eight years old; I don't know how people are supposed to die. Susie died by drowning when she couldn't swim. Tanairí said maybe she died in the trunk of the car because she couldn't breathe with the plastic bag, and it was too hot for her. Perhaps I can drown myself to death. If I jump on the deepest side of the pool, I will drown just like Susie did.

Without hesitation I jumped in the pool and kept going up and down. I want to stay down, but my body keeps pushing back up. It's not a good feeling, but it doesn't hurt. I can feel my heart pounding in my head; it starts loud, but quickly the sound fades away. Everything goes slowly. I'm neither going up much nor gasping for air. My eyes close while turning off the camera. Suddenly, I cough and throw up water. My eyes are open, and I'm lying on the floor in the middle of a circle with everyone staring at me and the lifeguard all soaked in water next to me. I hear the chaperone telling me to stay with her. She helps me to my feet and holds my hand. She says, Let's go to the park instead.

I kept silent the rest of the day. My mouth stays shut, and so do my thoughts. Just like my sisters, I failed. I am slightly disheartened by my inability to achieve death. Why did someone have to be a hero and rescue me? Now I understand why Tanairí got mad at me. I also feel betrayed for being saved.

I'm learning how to be quieter now. I don't talk as much as before. People think that I'm shy; they make remarks about it and ask me if a mouse bit my tongue. How ironic; no one wants to hear me, and they also wonder why I'm quiet. Maybe I have nothing to say.

Other times I feel the urge to scream. When I scream, I get a relief sensation; it's like letting all my feelings come out at once. I like that I don't remember anything for a few minutes. My mind gets a break, and all my thoughts stay still. It is not something that I can control or decide when to do. I always get this sick feeling; my heart starts racing, and I can't breathe. I'm keeping so many secrets that I choke on them. When I scream, I safely tell my secrets, because I know no one will ever hear the words hidden in my scream.

I still go and exchange a list with my dad for food. I go to Manny and to all those nameless men my mom sends me to. My mom still goes out for days at a time. I usually go and look after her. Sometimes I find her, and sometimes I don't. Sometimes she comes home with me, and other times she slaps me in the face and tells me that she is the one in control—not me. I feel sorry for Leilani, so I make my brother happy, so she doesn't have to be scared and hide all the time. Therefore, every day I do something to pay my dues. I hate having to do business. I hate businessmen!

Pending Message

4

No one looked on you with pity or had compassion enough
to do any of these things for you.
Rather, you were thrown out into the open field,
for on the day you were born, you were despised.

Ezekiel 16:5 NIV

I turned nine years old, and my mother didn't even say happy birthday to me. She never does. She always forgets; she says she has too many kids to keep up with it. I'm used to it by now, but still, I feel sad and rejected. She slapped me again and told me I shouldn't tell her when to come home. She had just come out of the drug house smoking a thin cigarette. Jose was with her, and when she slapped me, they both started making fun of me. I told her I'm going home, but next time she slaps me, I'm running away for good.

She says I need to go to church because I'm disrespectful. She already talked to a woman who will pick me up on Sunday. Why? I asked. She replied, because you don't learn, and you need help. Either God punishes you, or God will make you a better person. I hope he punishes you for being stubborn.

On Sunday, she woke me up early, gave me a shower, and brushed my hair. Then she kicked me out of the house because she didn't want the woman to invite her to church. I stood in the front yard for a long time, waiting for someone I didn't even know. While I waited, I ate breakfast, a buffet of leaves from the plants in the yard.

A woman named Marianela finally came and took me to church. Everybody seemed to know each other, which made me feel even more uncomfortable. For once, I was the stranger. An old lady handed me a tambourine to play with, and I didn't know how to. She came back and told me to close my eyes. No! I won't shut my eyes. I'm afraid. What if I close my eyes and a man touches me? I've never been here before. I don't know where the monsters are hiding. While the pastor preached, I only heard one part: "God loves every man." At the end of his sermon, he asked people to come to the altar to pray, and that same woman came back and practically pushed me to the front. You need to kneel and pray, she said.

So, I kneeled at the altar, lay my head on the steps, and cover my face with my arms so no one could see that my eyes are still open. I'm not closing them!

Dear God, why are you so mean? I asked you to forgive me. I've been waiting for almost two years, and you never showed up. Because of you, no one loves me. You make them hate me. The mother you gave me won't forgive me unless you do. The father you gave me abandoned me just like you did here on earth. I was scared to come to church because I'm afraid of you. But I thought maybe, if I came to your house, you would finally listen. This is your house, isn't it? Yet, you're just like my mom. You needed a break and left. Where are you, God? Did you hear what the pastor said? Well, God, the man you love so much touches me. You love men and not the women? That's why you punish me and not them. Everyone turns away just like you. I will never come back to this place again. God, I hope you punish everyone else like you're punishing me. With no mercy. If I don't die and I get to grow up, I promise I'll kill the old lady for being annoying, and I'll kill the pastor too. If he wants to deliver your message, maybe he should preach to a church full of men, not just old ladies. Above all, I'll kill every single man who has touched me. Then perhaps you'll get my message.

When I stood up, I knew it was a mistake to be disrespectful to God. I know He is going to punish me and send me to hell. My breath shortens, and I feel dizzy. The pastor says, "God is here!" and everyone gets excited. But I get so scared, and I pass out. The church thinks it was the touch of God. If only they knew it wasn't God who I felt; it was terror.

Emilia and Oswaldo moved to the United States, and I don't miss them at all. But Mara misses him and has been looking for someone to replace him with. I went out with Mara, and this man standing at the bus terminal started whistling at her. I hate seeing men whistle at women; it feels like they're calling a dog. That's how Mom calls us when she leaves our food on the floor at the top of the stairs, with her signature whistling. Mara likes any attention she can get from men. One hour later, there's a new stranger in the house, and right away she takes him into her bedroom. My mother meets him, and I can tell she's not impressed by him. Still, he spends the night in our home.

Since the first day we met him, he became my new threat. He would kiss Mara and call me over for me to watch how they kissed and touched each other. Then they would laugh and make fun of me for not wanting to watch. They said I was just jealous that he chose her and not me to be his girlfriend. My mother heard them making fun of me, but she didn't care. Her only response to my complaints was, It should only bother you if what they're saying is true; is it true?

I didn't want to watch my sister act in a real-life porn movie. Having to watch them was disgusting. But that became the new normal. They would have sex, and I had to watch them. Mara and Michael would ask me to join them. Then they'd keep mocking me. Do you like this? We know you want us to do this to you. Don't be jealous; you're ugly compared to Mara, but you can join us. Look, I have enough for both of you. You can drink both from it. When we're done, we'll buy you an ice cream cone so you can practice for next time. We know you're crying because Mara got it all and didn't leave anything for you. Next time, you can have it all.

My mother got into a relationship with an old, grumpy man. She's always sitting on the men's lap, kissing and putting on a show; this one is no exception. When she drinks alcohol, her personality changes completely. She becomes a sex idol, and every other female becomes her competition. Her daughters must not obstruct her radiant aura when she's in that state of drunkenness. She comes home and cooks' dinner for him, acting like he is a god. When she cooks for him, it's only for him. He brings her food and says, that's for you; don't share it with those ugly girls. I never ask for food, and my sisters wouldn't dare. I feel sorry for my little sister, Leilani. She's still innocent and doesn't understand how to play my mother's game. Mom will hit you until you prove it doesn't hurt anymore. When you match her strength, she gives up. I will beat her.

The man from the gambling house was right; it's my food. If I pay a high price for it, then I'll hide it from my brother and my mother. I often take my little sister around the neighborhood to play. If I get money, I'll buy her food. I want to teach her how to survive, but I think her eyes are still closed.

Mom's new boyfriend had a meeting, and only my sisters and brother were allowed to vote. He asked if they'd let him move into our house. They all said yes. My opinion didn't matter, so no one asked me. I raised my voice and complained. "Be quiet, I know you just want to ruin my happiness," Mom told me. But I guess he wanted to pretend he cared, so he finally asked for my vote. No, I said, and I ran to my room before Mom could slap me. My vote didn't matter, but I wanted to cast my vote. Who knows if this man is another hidden monster? Still, I now officially have a stepfather.

My brother still has episodes, but only during the day. Maybe he's afraid now that there's a new man who comes home late in the evening. There's constant friction between us. I ask myself, should I make him happy so my little sister won't get scared, or should I let him turn the house upside down? My mom still hits us for any little reason, if we talk too loudly or if we laugh. I'm not afraid of her anymore. I'm getting older and stronger. It doesn't hurt like it used to when she hits me. She uses the belt, the broom, her high heels, or whatever is within her reach. She'll even turn on the water hose to soak us when she comes home late to wake us up in the middle of the night. Other times, she throws rocks when she gets home drunk. I'm nine years old, and I'm learning how to survive. Hopefully, it won't take long for me to figure out how to die. All these Christians keep saying God is coming soon, but I don't think it's true.

If I do something to get on my mother's nerves, she sends me to church so God can punish me. She also says he can forgive me and make me better, but he hasn't. I'm terrified of God because of the punishments. I try not to bother her, even though it's inevitable. She gets mad for no reason or takes it out on me when she's having a bad day. Mom thinks I'm the one who's supposed to make everything better. Go shopping for her. Keep her son in a good mood. Every time she hits me, she says, I'm the mom, not you!

Hearing about God makes me sick. I think that's her weapon against me. I already wet my bed, and now when I know she's sending me to church, I throw up and poop myself in my sleep. Still, she wakes me up at dawn and makes me wait outside. I go to church to get punished. When I'm there, I get sick and dizzy. They always say God is there. But I've never felt peace in the middle of their chaos.

Tanairí thinks that Mom will change for the better. Since there's a man in the house, she might want to stay home to please him. Tanairí is our babysitter, so I understand why it would be good for her to have Mom around. I, on the other hand, am suffocating in her presence. She's not a better mom; she's a better woman. Our mother is playing housewife.

My little sister is in school, and I walk with her to school every day. I give her a hug and a goodbye kiss. I always tell her how beautiful she is. I want her to know she has a better chance in life. At home, I can't always protect her. Now we're having another sister, and Leilani won't be the baby anymore. Mom's getting mad at her for no reason, especially in the mornings before school. If she moves her head while getting her hair done, Mom will hit her on the head until the brush breaks into pieces. I stand in front of my sister so she can focus on me instead of the pain. We do a staring contest, and even if she loses, I let her win. I make silly faces and try to make her laugh, so she won't cry. I wish I could do her hair, but I don't know how. Mom doesn't want to deal with my curly hair either, so she cuts it like a boy's. Changes are coming, but I'd rather keep my role. I'm already used to doing business. I don't want Leilani to take my place.

Since Mom is pregnant, her partner thinks we're going to steal food, and she'll starve to death. Doesn't he know we can survive just by drinking water and eating ice cubes and leaves? He'll show the food and say, you see all that food? Well, it's not for you. I get the sense that he feels more important when he humiliates us, and my mother allows it. Our new stepfather enjoys telling us how ugly we are. Occasionally he pretends to be having a serious conversation, just to compare us to animals or monsters. My self-esteem is coming down.

I've never paid attention to my appearance, but now I find myself looking in the mirror. My stepfather says I'm ugly, and my mother laughs. She has never said I'm beautiful. The man who drives the public transportation, the one who squishes my hands, says my hands are small, and that alone makes him feel strong. I wish I could cut them off and stay with no hands. I've been thinking: how can I cut off my right hand without the left? Once I figure it out, I'll do it so he won't squish them ever again. I sometimes cover my hands with a piece of cloth. I put a needle through my skin, so the fabric stays in place, but my finger got infected. So, I stopped covering them.

I don't like my skin color; I have medium brown skin, and it makes me feel dirty. I don't like my eyes either; men are drawn to them, or so they say. I think they like to see my fear in them. I hate my curly, tangled hair; Mom says it's bad hair. I don't like my appearance. I wish I was beautiful, but what is a beautiful person even supposed to look like? If God ever forgives me and decides to make me better, does that mean he'll make me better physically or better in behavior? I haven't noticed whether Christians are attractive. Their judgmental attitude makes them ugly, but some of them are serene.

I asked my mother why she keeps having babies if she doesn't love the ones she already has. She said I have a big mouth and that people who talk too much get their tongues ripped apart. I ran to my room and hid under my bed; I didn't want her to cut my tongue off. She's been giving me silent treatment ever since. Still, I never got an answer to my honest question. I liked it better when she would leave us home alone for days at a time.

The baby has arrived; I have a new sister, the eighth in line. Tanairí is missing a lot of school because she has to babysit. I feel bad for her. She wakes up during the night to care for the baby and still has to go to school early in the morning, if she's even allowed to. Mom asked me to babysit, and I told her no. She offered me one dollar, but I still said no. What can I do with one dollar? Buy a soda can for my brother? The more babysitters she gets, the more babies she'll keep having. I've never seen her take care of my nieces or nephews. She always says, "If it's your baby, it's your responsibility." I will never be her personal babysitter! I take care of my dolls even though some are missing hair, arms, or legs. I still care for them. Toys are passed down from sister to sister. I already run errands and take care of my brother. Why should I do her more favors? I can't take care of a baby and calm my crazy brother at the same time.

 The tension is building, and I can feel it's only a matter of time before she punishes me. I won't babysit, no matter how many beatings I get or if she never speaks to me again. I'd rather live in fear in a church and become a nun. I'm not taking on Tanairí's role, and Leilani won't take mine. Here she comes again, asking me to help with the baby. No, I told her. She demanded that I do it, and the words slipped out of my mouth before I could stop them. The baby is your problem, not mine. Ask her dad to help you! I didn't even have a chance to apologize; her hand was already raised, and she slapped me across the face. When her hand came back to hit me again, I raised mine to stop hers. Reminding her, I told you next time you slap me, I will run away. I'm leaving this house today. Next time you lay a hand on me, I'll fight you. I will never forget the bad things you've done and the things you allowed others to do. One day, when I grow up, I'll write a book, and everyone will know who you are.

I stood in the front yard, thinking of where I could go. Luckily for me, my cousin passed by and invited me to her house. I told her I was running away, and she offered her home for me to stay. My aunt, on my dad's side, is nice. I enjoy spending time at her house with my cousins. She even tried everything to get legal custody of me. But I would rather not ruin her life the way I ruin everyone else's.

Emilia and Oswaldo keep calling. My mom bought me a plane ticket to send me to live with them in the United States. I don't want to go, but they keep telling me that my aunt would go to jail because of me. I am scared for her; she does not deserve that. My aunt took me to speak with a social worker, and my mother was already there, crying. It's the first time I had ever seen her cry. Does she cry too?

She told the social worker that my aunt is a bad person and my father an alcoholic. She even showed proof that I was supposed to be on medication. She said she was willing to fight for custody because my aunt had kidnapped me and taken advantage of my mental state. The social worker gave her a box of tissues. With tears in her eyes, she told the social worker how much she loved me. The social worker believed her and told me, you need to stop being a rebellious kid. You're making your mom suffer. You need to take your medication and attend school. If you keep misbehaving, do you know where we send bad kids? We send them to kids' jail. Do you want to go there? Tell your mom you love her and that you're sorry. I told the social worker I will never tell that woman I love her. Because I don't, she is not my mother.

I can't seem to get my message across to anyone, not even to God. They're all pending messages that no one wants to open.

A New Journey

5

Search me, O God, and know my heart;
test me and know my anxious thoughts.
Point out anything in me that offends you,
and lead me along the path of everlasting life.

Psalm 139:23-24 NLT

June 10, 1990, is a sunny, perfect day to travel. In the blink of an eye, I am once again in the claws of my mom, who is taking me to the airport. My heart is broken. I betrayed my aunt trying to protect her. It doesn't matter if she hates me; she's safe, and they won't be able to put her in jail. I get out of the car, pick up my bag and my plane ticket, and begin walking straight to the slaughterhouse. I feel in my heart I should run. Hide in a bathroom, then wander around the island. But I'm just a little girl. The smell of the ocean is trying to hold me back, and the hot weather is begging me not to go. Still, I take steps and follow the flight attendant into the plane.

The plane takes off, and everything stays behind. Puerto Rican flags wave goodbye. The houses look small, and cars turn into ants. I treasure in my heart the picture of this island that's disappearing right in front of me. The land where I was born, the one that fed me with her plants and entertained me with her waves. The land that knew me, even though I never truly knew her. A place full of beautiful places I've never seen. This small island raised warriors, the ones who fought with all their breath, and not even the conquerors could wipe them all out. This is where three races mixed into one, all of them leaving their footprints on me. I want to stay. This is where I belong.

Staring at the ocean, which is so big and never-ending, it separates my past from my future. As this gray bird keeps flying higher, now it looks like someone laid down a huge cotton blanket, and the bird flew above it. Devouring the white cotton candy sky, splitting the clouds in half. I'm in the clouds. Wait… I'm now closer to God!

God, now that you can hear me. I just want to apologize for all the bad things I did in heaven. Can I go back to heaven? Please, God.

I stay the whole flight looking out the window, wondering if God heard me, afraid to ask for a sign. I know He did; I'm so close to Him, floating above the clouds. Mom says I talk too much and need to learn how to be quiet. But now that I'm this close to God, I have so many things to tell Him, so many questions. Still, I need to prove to Him that I've learned my lesson. I will show God that I deserve to go back to heaven. The person sitting next to me asks for my name, but I ignore him. I will not talk while I'm on this plane. What if God says, *Shut up!* And gets mad? What if he throws this plane into the ocean? Maybe God likes silence. It's overwhelming when it's noisy.

I've been sitting in the same position for hours now, no talking, no movement, breathing as quietly as I can. People keep staring out their windows, amazed. The gray bird rocks gently from side to side, trying to stay balanced as we get closer to the city. Outside, I see neon lights shining like party decorations, rays of colors scattered across the night. It looks beautiful, but nothing like the island I left behind.

The plane has landed in the United States, and there's no turning back. I didn't want to live with my mom, but this place doesn't feel like home either. A boy around my age looks at me as if we're getting off and says, don't be scared. In the end, everything will be okay, and you'll talk. I just smile. Along with the plane, I've landed in a new place with new opportunities. I take a deep breath as I step off. Then reality hits, as I know who will be waiting is part of my family. That means I will still be trapped in a cage.

I walk down a long hallway, feeling alone and lost. Oswaldo is there, waiting with a friend. He wraps me with a hug while whispering, Welcome! I'm going to teach you many things.

The day after, my sister Emilia went over the rules of the house. I must obey them, no questions asked. I have to do all the house chores and help her with everything. It is prohibited to talk to God, since they have an Indian who is their protector, and he doesn't like it. I'm not allowed to talk to anyone. Not over the phone, not by mail, and not in person.

She takes me into her bedroom, which is right next to the living room, divided only by a curtain instead of a door. Her bedroom is full of candles. In the corner, she has what looks like an altar, a big plaster Indian statue surrounded by strange items and incense. There are knives in front of it, some clean, others dirty. She also has a plate of food and a cup of water. Her bedroom is small, with a dresser and a bed under the window. She invites me to sit on the bed and pull out some tarot cards. She divides them and asks me to choose a pack. I know how to read cards, she tells me. Emilia has always been odd; she enjoys hurting people in a way that makes them feel like they deserve it or even want it. She seems excited about the cards, just like she would get excited and laugh when she hurt someone.

She says, I see a handsome, strong man, and you must obey him in everything. He's going to ask you to be his girlfriend, and I'll tell you what he looks like so you will be able to recognize him. He has black eyes and curly hair, and his skin is darker than yours. Listen to me, you need to be his girlfriend. You cannot disobey what the cards are saying. Then she puts the cards away and tells me to stay where I am because she needs to ask me something important.

You owe us for rescuing you. Mom was going to send you to jail. She's tired of having to deal with you; she doesn't love you.

She already told us what you did. Be honest and tell me, what are the names of the guys who had sex with you behind the school? We know you're not a virgin.

I am confused over her questions. I guess Mom did call her. Why does she keep asking for the names of the guys behind the school? I don't know who they are. Besides, I didn't have sex with them. It wasn't me who stayed behind. What does she mean that I'm not a virgin? Well, I know that. Only those teenagers who died in the Catholic Church are virgins, and they make statues out of them. Some people pray to the statues because they believe the Virgin Mary can talk to her son and intercede with us humans. I think that's a waste of time. Why would God listen to a plaster statue and not to a living human? I'm not talking to anyone about that day behind the school. There are some flowers hiding in between the grass, and I promised to keep them secret. I don't want them to be stepped on.

My sister keeps talking and asking. I keep ignoring her. It makes me feel sick to talk about bad things. She keeps going on, telling me the story of how she bled on the sheets the first time she had sex with her ex-husband, Eddy. I tell her I don't care, and I don't want to talk about those things. She just laughs and says, you'll care soon.

I would rather play with my niece and nephews, but she wants me here listening to her stories. Oswaldo puts on some Santería music, and it's louder than my sister's voice. He comes and takes me to the living room and tells me to stay standing. He cooked something that made a lot of smoke and stink up the house; Emilia passed it to him. He keeps going in circles around me, trapping me in the middle of the smoke. He says, this will prepare me for the special day.

They don't make sense. I obey, being still. I don't make a sound; I breathe softly. I'm practicing how to be quiet and keep the words to myself. Silence is the proof that I learned my lesson. I don't know if God is looking for me, but if He is, this time I will behave in heaven.

As the days pass, I get more used to them. Oswaldo sells drugs, just like he used to do in Puerto Rico. Now it's my job to look out the window and let him know if the police are driving by. Since she doesn't want to get in trouble if the house gets raided, Emilia leaves with her three children. This apartment is dirty with countless cockroaches everywhere you look. My sister doesn't like to clean, so I do it for her. It's difficult to sweep a rug with an old broom. I'm not allowed to use the vacuum, and the broom keeps losing plastic bristles that get stuck in the carpet. But that doesn't stop me. I'm determined to clean this dumpster.

My sister loves to eat at McDonald's with her kids; she always takes them there. She barely cooks; I'm not even sure if she knows how to. I don't get hungry that often anyway. Usually, a glass of water fills me up. At dinner, I have to wait for everyone else to be served. First, they give food to the Indian statue in the bedroom. Then Oswaldo gets his plate, followed by his oldest son because he's the favorite, then the youngest son because he's a boy. My sister and her daughter came next. If there's anything left over anything Oswaldo doesn't want, then I can eat. I'm only allowed to eat standing up. My sister says my legs are too skinny and that eating while standing might help the food go to my legs. By the time it's my turn, the food is cold, and it doesn't taste good. Seeing the roaches and hearing my sister make fun of me takes away my hunger. My stepfather used to talk about my hair and my face. It turns out that my whole body is ugly.

They keep talking about my birthday and how special that day will be. They seem more excited than me. I wonder if they'll have a cake. It would be the first time someone had given me a birthday cake. The first time someone remembered or acknowledged my day. My mother always forgets my birthday. Now that I mention her, she hasn't even called to ask if I'm okay or behaving. Oh well. My birthday is coming soon, and I'm starting to believe it might actually be a special day.

It's a hot summer day at the beginning of August, and I miss the fresh breeze from Puerto Rico. Here it's so humid I can feel the vapor rising from the tar. There are barely any trees, just a few planted in a perfect pattern, each one fenced off in a tiny square. If my life depended on trees, I'd be dead soon. I'm always expected to go with Oswaldo when he runs errands or sells drugs. He says the police won't search a girl, so I have to carry the drugs. But it doesn't make sense for the police to stop him when he brings drugs to a cop. James is a tall, blond-haired American officer with blue eyes. We see him in uniform, driving his police car. Other times we go to his house. He has a wife and two sons. His wife is very thin, with short, curly blond hair. Occasionally, he slaps her across the face in front of us, just like my mother used to slap me.

Today we met with James to bring him drugs. On the way back home, we stopped at a video store. Oswaldo picked out a cartoon movie for his son and a porn movie for him and Emilia. The heat is unbearable, and it feels like there's no air to breathe. Even though I don't like being at their house, it's better than being outside. We live on the fourth floor, and there's no yard to play in. The apartment only has two bedrooms, one for my sister and Oswaldo and one for the three kids and me.

There are no doors, just curtains. The bathroom is inside the kids' room, so there's no privacy. From the living room windows, I can see the tall buildings and cars on North Fourth Street. It's boring here. The kid's bedroom has a single window facing the back, where the fire escape leads down to the dumpsters. Even though the dumpsters are outside, it looks cleaner than the inside of this apartment.

We were climbing the stairs when Oswaldo blocked my path. He stopped mid-step, trapping me with his arms. Do you want to be my girlfriend? He asked. No, I said. He smirked. Don't worry, your sister knows and agrees with our relationship. No! I don't want to be your girlfriend. I'm nine years old, and you're my brother-in-law. I felt disgusted. Isn't that why you came to live with us? He asked. Don't you want to be my girlfriend, like Mara?

I tried pushing him away, but he was stronger. He leaned closer, his face almost touching mine, and whispered, when we go upstairs, I'll tell Emilia you said no. Then he kissed me on the mouth. I shoved him again and finally broke free, running up to the apartment.

I thought he'd keep it a secret. But the moment he stepped inside, he told her, like a whining child throwing a tantrum. Emilia! He shouted. You better do something about your sister. I asked her to be my girlfriend, and she said no. If she doesn't agree, I don't want her here. Look at that worthless girl. She's had sex with so many men, and she doesn't even know how to kiss.

Emilia burst out laughing like it was the funniest thing she'd heard. I stood frozen. Then suddenly, her laughter stopped.

She called me into her room, and as soon as I walked in, she beat me up. You whore! I told you to obey. I told you a cute guy would ask you to be his girlfriend, and you were supposed to say yes. That's why Mom gave up on you. You're worthless! She shouted, pulled my hair, and hit me over and over.

According to my sister, I'm now Oswaldo's girlfriend, even though I clearly said no. I guess that doesn't matter. She says all men cheat, and it's better he cheats with me than with someone else. She's afraid of HIV and tells me that because I'm not sick, I'm the safe choice. If you love me, you'll do this, she says. You don't want me to die, do you? Over and over, she insists that I accept. To her, keeping it in the family means no one has to find out. It will be just another secret we'll all carry. Mara was his girlfriend before me, and they got along. Emilia says women become mistresses all the time for gifts and special treatment. At least this way, she says, he won't spend money on gifts, and she won't be exposed to any disease.

Oswaldo sometimes plays with me. He pretends in front of his kids to tickle me, and I don't like it. When he tickles me, he tends to touch my private parts; he grabs my small breasts and puts his hands in between my legs. I pushed him away and told him to stop. He always complains to my sister. She then will join him in the game. She held me down with strength so I wouldn't move and for him to tickle and touch me. I don't understand what the point of their game is. She holds me down so hard that it hurts me. The scary part is that she is the one who enjoys the game. Especially when he touches me. I know she likes it because of her facial expression and smile.

There are a few occasions when my niece shares with me her dollies, and we engage in play. I try to play with my nephews, but their father always ruins the fun. He says that boys need to learn how to be the man of the house and tells them to hit me so they can learn how to be dominant and take control.

I went with Emilia to register for school. Classes start in September, and my nephew Junior is starting kindergarten. The three of us will attend Lauer's Park Elementary in Reading, Pennsylvania. Emilia bought new clothes for her kids, then took me to a thrift store. She said I didn't deserve anything new because I'm not her daughter, and as Oswaldo's mistress, I shouldn't look better than her.

My birthday is coming up, and Oswaldo is keeping a countdown. Maybe birthdays are special in the United States. Emilia eats cake and ice cream often. I still have to eat standing up, and after two months, my legs look the same. It has been two months since my mother sent me to a "new life," but nothing has really changed, except that now I run errands with my brother-in-law and not alone.

A new journey, they said. But I recognize this road; it still hurts the same. I thought I was traveling alone, but now I realize that hell followed me. I no longer deal with the businessmen, so perhaps I should be grateful. I'm still locked in a cage, but somehow, I'm free. I'm not responsible for my brother anymore.

A Birthday Gift

6

The watchmen found me as they made their rounds
in the city. They beat me, they bruised me;
they took away my cloak, those watchmen of the walls!

Songs of Solomon 5:7 NIV

It's August twenty-seventh, nineteen ninety. Today is my tenth birthday. My sister woke up in a good mood, playing music early and loud like they usually do in Puerto Rico on Saturdays, but today's Monday. Without being asked, I start cleaning the house. Even on my birthday, it's my duty to help and earn the food they give me. To be honest, today is not relevant to me. They've said so much that I lost interest. The whole thing became annoying, just like them.

Emilia is ready early, dressing her boys as they wake up. Oswaldo says with excitement, It's your birthday! You'll get a special present! Emilia rushes the kids, planning to go out for breakfast and then to the city park. I admit, it feels good that someone remembers my birthday. I rush to finish cleaning and get dressed. I have only a few clothes in a cardboard box, so picking an outfit is easy.

Finally, we're ready! I head out the door until Emilia stops me by putting her hand on my chest. Where do you think you're going? You're staying here with Oswaldo to be on the lookout. Then you'll get your present. Enjoy the surprise; you'll love it. She says it with excitement, like she's the one enjoying the moment.

I clean the table and get the scale and plastic bags ready. When my brother-in-law starts working with the drugs, I kneel by the window hidden. I watch and take notes on who comes and goes. As I look out, I wonder what McDonald's breakfast tastes like. Mom used to say those places were for the privileged. My sister goes often. I've been inside with them, but I am not allowed to eat. I just watch them, not worthy enough to have any. My sister is the one who eats the food from my Happy Meal, and my nephew gets the surprise toy.

Once he finishes putting his drugs in their individual bags, he tells me to go into his bedroom to find my birthday present. I walked in, and there's nothing out of the ordinary. I came out, and Oswaldo is laughing at me, asking if I found it. I tell him there's nothing, but he swears it's in the room. He keeps insisting, and I give it one more try. I was expecting a box, a balloon, or maybe a small piece of cake. Perhaps I need to look for something smaller.

The big candles are lit, the Indian is standing tall with a dead pigeon at his feet, and bloody knives are scattered around him. Still, there's nothing big or small, so I give up. He's waiting in the living room and starts laughing when he sees me come out empty-handed. You are so stupid, he tells me. Your present is on the bed. How can you not see it? I go back in, and there's still nothing. Thinking he must be messing with me, I'm done searching. I walk to the kitchen because the dishes should be dry by now and need to be put away.

Oswaldo grabs my arm and says he'll help me find the present, practically pushing me into his bedroom. He keeps mocking me. It's on the bed; don't you see it? I feel stupid for even thinking someone might care about me, as if this day wasn't already cursed. There's nothing special about it. I try to walk away, but he blocks the entrance to his room. He then grabs my face and kisses me. I push him away when he tries again. I refuse to be his girlfriend, even though my sister insists that I already am.

Don't tell me you don't want this. After all, you came from Puerto Rico to be with me. I've waited two months to make this day special. I promise you'll never forget it. You will remember this day for the rest of your life. From now on, you belong to me, he says.

I don't want any present; Emilia can have it. I came here because I was sent; I had no choice. Can you please let me leave your room? As I try to walk away one more time, he grabs me by the arm. I tried to threaten him: I'll tell my sister that you're hurting me.

Go ahead and tell her, he said. Your sister knows you're getting your birthday present, and so does your mom. You still came from Puerto Rico; you wanted this all along. I attempt to break free, but his grip tightens. He gets angry and slams me onto his bed. He lies on top of me and attempts to kiss me. Whispering, it's your fault; you wanted this. I know you want this as much as I do. It's your fault!

While he's on top of me, he starts pulling off my clothes. I pushed him, but not hard enough to escape. He gets even more aggressive and slaps me across the face. Time starts to twist, moving too slowly and too fast all at once. In the blink of an eye, I'm naked. Time has betrayed me. He stands next to the bed and starts undressing. The white T-shirt, blue jeans, and white briefs, while looking at me like a serpent, licking his lips. Please! I beg you, do not look at my naked body. But like a broken record, he keeps repeating, It's your fault. You want this. It's your fault.

- Oswaldo, I don't want this. Let me put my clothes on. Let me go!

He climbs back on top of me, and I scream, No! I don't want this. Let me go! I try to crawl into the corner of the bed, but I've already hit the headboard; there's nowhere else to go. He grabs me by the hair and throws me down again.

I scream in an attempt to escape, and he stops. He asked me, you want people to hear you? While he walks to the window and opens it. Let's see who cares about you now. Go ahead. Scream all you want.

He lies back on me, and I keep fighting. He keeps slapping me and yanking my hair. It becomes a cycle, on repeat, and it feels like it will never end. The window is wide open, but no one hears me. Isn't my scream louder than the Santeria music playing in the background? Who can help me when no one wants to hear?

He got up from the bed and dragged me with him by the hair. He had overpowered me. Grabbing a few pillows, he placed them near the footboard and pushed me back onto the bed, stuffing the pillows under my hips. He muttered in frustration, you are so little.

He lay on top of me, and I felt this horrible pain. Instantly a scream escaped from my lips, and my legs began to shake. That made him angry. He stood up, grabbed a knife from the top of his dresser, and pressed it against my face. The blade was stained with old blood from the little bird he had killed. I could feel the tip of the knife on my right cheek, just under my eye.

If you move, you'll stab yourself, he warned me as if he cared about me. I'll try one last time. If you don't stay still, if you don't stop your legs from shaking, I'll give your blood to the Indian, and no one will ever know you're dead. I will place your body on a dish. I held my legs down with all the strength I had left. Then I turned my face to the left, away from the knife, toward the open window.

The pain came again, but I had to stop my body from shaking. I didn't close my eyes anymore. I forced myself to become a robot. I'm scared, and it hurts.

I can smell him; he's sweating. He keeps whispering, It's your fault. It's the way you look at me, the way you smile. You are making me do this; it's your fault!

Today is a hot, sunny day. The clouds are slowly moving; they look white and fluffy, like cotton candy. Somewhere up in the skies, there's a castle; I know it. A castle that no one can find and no one can enter. A place with strong stone walls that no one can break into. If I run fast enough on top of the clouds, I know I can reach it. I must run, and I cannot fall. Then I will be safe. I need to run away.

Brenda, you stupid whore! I hear his voice from far away. Once I stop running on the clouds, they immediately disappear from under my feet, and as they do, it makes me fall back into reality. Forcing me to land back on the bed. As my eyes open, I see him standing fully dressed. Go to the bathroom and wash yourself, he demanded.

He helped me walk to the bathroom because my body wouldn't respond when I tried to walk. The bathtub was already filled with water. "Wash yourself," he says. I sat on the bathtub, feeling like all of my emotions got on a roller coaster ride together. I can feel all of them at once while feeling emotionless at the same time. I can't comprehend what just happened, nor how I am feeling about it.

He is asking me to cleanse myself, but there's no way to do it. He keeps entering the bathroom to make sure I'm washing, but I just can't. I'm scrubbing my body, and it doesn't get clean. I am dirty.

As soon as I get out of the bathtub, I get dressed. Afraid that he'll come back and do it again if he sees that I'm naked. Oswaldo comes into the bedroom holding a white extension cord with his hands and tells me to go to the living room. I was still crossing the line between the bedroom and the living room, and he was already pushing me into a corner. Since you don't want to move in bed, you won't move around the house either, he says. He sat me on the floor and tied my hands and feet with the extension cord, like they do to hostages in the movies. It hurts, but I'm not saying a word. I'd rather stay quiet.

Emilia came home and saw me on the floor. She thought it was funny. When she finally caught her breath from laughing, she asked, What's wrong? You didn't like your surprise? I begged her to untie me. It was too tight, and it hurt, but she simply said no. She's mad at me, and I don't know why. They ordered Chinese food for dinner. My sister asked if I was hungry, and I said yes. So, she threw some rice on the floor and told me to eat it like a dog. Oswaldo got mad because she threw rice. He said, Give her the bones instead.

She started shouting at me because I wasn't eating. I'm going to beat you up if you don't eat from the floor, she threatened. Then she asked Oswaldo to have sex with me again. I quickly licked the rice off the floor. The bones too, she added, mocking me as I ate. After I finished, I began to weep. My hands and feet were in so much pain, it felt like they were going to explode from the tightness of the extension cord, and I thought maybe if I cry, the blood will come out through my eyes. As I cried, I kept checking my tears to see if they had any blood in them.

I wish God would tell me what I did in heaven to deserve such punishment here on earth. I couldn't have done something like this to an angel. God, please forgive me! I scream in my mind because I don't want them to hear me. Hoping for God to hear my scream telepathically. God, where are you? Please come and get me.

I've been sitting on the floor for hours, thinking I have telepathic powers, while having conversations with God in my mind. But He doesn't seem to hear me. I must be going crazy. God should be the last person on my mind, yet He's the one I desperately need. I imagine an invisible person shielding me, and that thought alone comforts me. Then reality hits, and here I am, alone, hopeless, like a wounded dog. God, please rescue me.

Why doesn't Emilia shut her mouth? She keeps talking about the same thing. When I had sex with Eddy for the first time, I bled; there was blood on the sheets. Look, there's no blood on these. That's the proof you were not a virgin. Everyone bleeds the first time. The sheets are clean; I don't have to wash them, she repeats nonstop. It's almost bedtime, and I'm still tied up on the floor waiting for the punishment to end. The pain in my feet and hands last for a short time, then goes numb. Eventually, I forget about the pain. I'm thirsty, but I don't dare ask for water. It's better to stay quiet, to be still, like a robot. My sister is watching her soap opera; I cannot interrupt.

Maybe if I ask Oswaldo, he'll have pity on me. Yes! He just stood up. Can you please untie me? It hurts. Look, my hands and feet are going to explode. Please. He just stared at me, and I could hear my sister in the background saying no. He sat on the floor next to me to untie me and released me from my punishment.

The person who threatened to give my blood to the Indian and serve my body on a plate is now showing me mercy at night. I went from fear, disappointment, and hate to feeling grateful for his pity.

He asked me to go to sleep. Unable to stand on my feet, I did a low crawl, like a soldier, as fast as I could to cross that line from the living room to the bedroom. Wishing to close my eyes just this one time. I need a mind reset to delete today's memory. Instead, I cry to sleep. Knowing deep in my soul that today I was marked forever. Thinking he was right, today is a date I will never forget.

I should be feeling full of energy and excited. Cuddling with a doll or a stuffed animal until I fall asleep. Thinking about how much I enjoyed the day and planning for tomorrow's play. Since school starts in a few days, look at the new clothes and choose an outfit. Maybe complaining about the weather, tossing around in bed trying to find the coolest spot. But instead, I feel exhausted and confused. Not understanding what happened today or why I couldn't find the castle. Afraid of what tomorrow will look like. I can't stand the heat; I can't breathe. I hate the sunny, hot days because people sweat, and it's disgusting. I'm dirty; I was unable to clean myself. God, where are you? I looked for your house, and I couldn't find it. I fell from the clouds; you kicked me out of heaven. Where are you? Now I am dirty, and I can't go back. What did I do to deserve this?

Still, today was my birthday, and I should be grateful that someone remembered for the first time. Happy birthday to me!

School started, and it's very hard for me to learn in school. I don't speak English, so most of the time, I'm lost. I'm not allowed to talk to the teachers or to have friends. They all think I'm shy, and that's why I don't participate in conversations. If only they would ask if there was something I had to say, but I learned a long time ago that no one really cares. At lunch, some days I swallow my food, afraid it'll be taken away from me. Other days, I space out, and before I realize it, it's time for me to go back to class, and I stay hungry until the next day. At home my food portion is very limited, if I'm lucky.

I asked the teacher if I could get extra homework and receive a pad instead of a grade. The teacher refused and told me to ask my mom to purchase some instead. But I always figure something out. Now I steal napkins or toilet paper from the school bathroom or any public place and use them during my menstrual cycle. On weekends, I sometimes have to reuse them, and since I'm not allowed to discard them at home, I store them in my backpack until I return to school, where I can throw them away. In moments like this, I'm glad people see me as the shy girl. Like my backpack, I carry plenty of dirty secrets.

The first time I asked Emilia for a pad, she beat me up and said I was disgusting for having a period. I'm allowed one pad a day. I also get punished when Oswaldo wants to have sex with me, and I'm on those days. So, I try to hide it from them as long as I can. Wishing I could control when it happens. Oswaldo sometimes shows me pity. He'll say things like; I won't have sex with you until two days after you're done. I'll take care of you. You can have something sweet or juice. Here, I got you two extra pads. The things other girls my age take for granted are privileges for me. Yes, I'm grateful for his pity.

My sister is scarier than her husband. She blames me for not knowing how to please him. She seems to enjoy when he has sex with me. She orders takeout food and gets in a better mood. The crazy thing is that she will also beat me up when she's happy. The only thing that changes is the expression on her face. Excited or mad, she expresses both through hitting me. I don't know how to please her. She is like our brother, a ticking time bomb. If I laugh or cry, she tells him it is because I want sex. I'm learning how to keep my emotions neutral. I don't laugh or cry unless they require me to. I avoid eye contact with men to keep from attracting attention. I stopped smiling; now I remain silent. My mom would be proud.

Every time my brother-in-law has sex with me, I get punished. Supposedly, I don't please him, and my sister thinks I'm pretending. The truth is, I don't know what to do. So, I ran on top of the clouds, trying to find the castle. If it exists, then I need to find it. I want to know what the inside looks like. Are the walls inside made of stone, like the ones on the outside? Are there secret passageways for emergencies? Soldiers dressed in armor, ready to protect the people inside? I need to know how safe I'll be once I get in.

My sister doesn't understand that I don't want to be her husband's girlfriend. Just because Mara liked him doesn't mean I will. I want to be a normal girl, like the ones at school. To have clothes to talk about and different hairstyles. Make plans during lunch about which TV show to watch and ask for a new toy after seeing the commercial. Wishing to experience having my first boyfriend. To get a little note with the question, "Do you want to be my girlfriend?" Then decide where to put the check mark on yes or no. It must be nice to draw a heart on a piece of paper, smile through the school morning, and cry at lunchtime because the relationship lasted only a few hours. All of those experiences were stolen from me.

Today I wasn't allowed to go to school; Emilia has an appointment, and he said this is the perfect chance to have the house for us. I begged my sister to let me go with her, but as usual, she turned her back on me. I told him while I was crying that I hate him.

As soon as we are home alone, he takes me into the bedroom. He tried to kiss me, and I moved my face to the other side. Again, he tried, and I moved away. Grabbing my face, he kissed me. I hate kissing! I don't like it when people touch my face. I hate the feeling of a hand on my face. Anger overtook me; I pushed and threatened him. Next time I see the police, I will tell them that you kissed me. He got mad, hit me, and still had sex with me. He hurt me because I didn't behave, and I deserved it. After my sister arrived, they spent hours talking in their bedroom.

He went out to pick up the kids from school and brought a big cardboard box. He asked me to go inside the box with his older son. Then he asked us to kiss and touch each other in our private parts. We didn't; my nephew is now crying because he asked him to be a man, unless he was homosexual and wanted a boy inside the box instead of me. As time passed, we were both tired and sweating. I gave up and convinced my nephew to kiss and touch me so he could go out to eat and play. He did, and we were free from the box. Oswaldo told me, You are just like me! You kissed your nephew. If you talk, then I will also tell them, and we will both go to jail.

I thought I wasn't a monster, and I turned out to be exactly like them. It's like someone wrapped the extension cord around my heart. At ten years old I received a birthday gift that marked me forever.

To Be Punished

7

My tears have been my food day and night,
while people say to me all day long,
Where is your God?

Psalm 42:3 NIV

My brother-in-law is looking for another girlfriend. He's been going out to the nightclubs and coming home late at night. There are always arguments between him and my sister. He is spending time with a teenage girl from high school. She is older than me and more on the popular side. I truly hope their relationship lasts; presently, she is my only hope. I'm getting a break from him.

Because Emilia doesn't want to get sick, she insists it's better for him to have an affair with me. She says if he gets sick, then I will get sick too. She is terrified that he will leave her for someone else. Therefore, she wants me to make him fall in love. Though my opinion has never been valued by anyone, I would rather not do such a thing. She also told me that I should have a baby, and if I give birth to a girl, I will be treated like a princess.

He comes from a family of twelve brothers, and he has two sons. She could be the first girl for his family, and they would love her. Emilia also has this plan for protecting me when I become pregnant. She will keep me hidden until I give birth. If I have a daughter, she will raise her as her own. They don't need more boys; therefore, if I give birth to one, she will kill him and pour his blood on the Indian statue just like they do with the little animals. No one will ever find out. His body will be eaten by the worms until there's nothing left.

My sister's mood varies from one moment to another. From being happy and excited, she turns into a monster ready to destroy me. I'm afraid I do not wish to have his child. My sister thinks it is the only way to keep him by her side. She is excited about the idea of breaking the news. Based on this calendar she is following, on certain days, her husband needs to have sex with me so I can get pregnant. It feels more like a ritual of old wives' tales.

This morning, I wrote a letter to my mother asking about the weather and my sisters. The breeze in Puerto Rico made me feel like I wasn't alone. It was like being covered; I miss its warmth. The trees took care of me; they didn't let me go hungry. Here, it's getting cold, and the leaves are falling from the trees. It seems like the wind is forcing them to get naked. Emilia said she was going to buy me a stamp so I could send the letter by mail, but in exchange, I need to beg Oswaldo not to go out tonight. I begged, just like she asked me, and he stayed home.

It's the middle of the night, and everyone is sleeping. He came into my room, woke me up, and took me to the bathroom. You wanted me to stay, didn't you? You're jealous of me being with someone else? He asked while undressing me. He turned on the water and let it run. You want this, he whispered. For some reason, the water sounds too loud, and it hurts my ears. I don't like the steam rising from the tub; it makes me feel nauseated. I try to ignore the sound, but then I can hear him breathing behind me. That sound fills me with rage. I stare at the water running and filling the bathtub. Water is supposed to clean me when I shower, but it never does. I feel angry. I wonder how deep the water is. Could I drown in there?

While I'm lost in that thought, he pulls me by the hair and drags me back to reality. Go lie on your back, he says. You're not allowed to shower. He always asks me to shower after he's done using me, and it's the only thing that gives me some relief. Now that's being taken away. I dare to ask, why can't I shower? He replies, because you're getting pregnant. He grabs me by the arms and practically throws me onto my bed. He takes the pillows and shoves them under my hips. Go to sleep and don't move, he says. I'll be watching. Don't move.

I stayed awake after he sent me to sleep. He only uses pillows to raise me up because I'm little. He left for his bedroom and spoke with my sister. They laughed, and then I think they fell asleep. I stayed still, waiting for him to come back. Not because I wanted him to return, but because I was terrified that he would. I felt nauseous. He didn't let me shower, and the feeling of filth was sickening.

Emilia woke up early and got the kids ready to go out. They usually go for breakfast on Saturdays. I stayed here to keep an eye out for the police and to be his partner. It's always the same routine. They play loud music, and I clean the disgusting house. I help him set up the table and then kneel in front of the window. When he finishes preparing the drugs, he takes me to the bedroom. I think I'm getting used to it. As soon as he put away the drugs, he told me I could take a quick shower. Finally. I had been feeling so dirty since the night before. I ran to the bathroom, and before I could rinse the soap off, he walked in. I'm not even allowed to lock the door.

Once I'm done, he takes me to his bedroom. Why do I try to be clean? He told me, from now on, you will only shower before we have sex. I want to cry. Every time I feel shattered, they find another piece of me to break. I keep my tears inside, even though I feel that I'm drowning with them; I am heartbroken. As he opens the window, I lie down on his bed without resisting or being asked to. He tells me I can scream all I want. I don't scream anymore; I know no one cares, and if I do, he'll hit me. Instead, I go searching for the castle. I'm confident I'll find it one day. I run away to the clouds before I feel the pain. I always feel pain when he lies on top of me, and my legs still shake uncontrollably.

I was about to take it off when someone knocked on the door. He covered my mouth with his hand and whispered, If I go to jail, you will go too. Whoever it was kept knocking, and he panicked. Put your clothes on quick, he said, while he also got dressed. Stay here; don't move. He answered the door, and it was a man. I could hear them talking. Oswaldo came back into the house and told me to wait for him in the living room, then he left.

For the first time, I was home alone, and I didn't know what to do. I peeked through the window and saw him get into a car. I'm alone. I ran to his bedroom to grab the gun. I wanted to shoot myself in the head, but he took it. Should I take a shower? Eat something so I won't starve until Monday? Should I cry myself to sleep? I want to do so many things, but every option is only temporary. I'm tired of being punished by life, of being mocked, ignored, and rejected. I'm tired of living. Looking down from the window, I wonder what will happen if I jump. Will I die? Will it be the end of me?

I opened the window and thought, If I run fast enough, straight from the door, I will fall right through. I moved everything out of the way and stood in front of the door. I will jump from the fourth-floor window. I started to run, and about halfway, I fell to the floor. I feel defeated. How can I fall at this moment? This is my only chance, probably the only time I'll be left alone, and I fall. Why do I always need to fall when I have to run? From the floor, I can see the clouds through the open window. I wonder if God doesn't want me to die.

What can I do? There's nothing left but to cry. Drowning in my tears, I say, God, please help me! And as always, time betrayed me: four words, and I was no longer home alone.

My sister arrived home in the evening. Oswaldo beat her up and then left the house. When he left, she beat me up and said, It's your fault!

The kids went to sleep early, and so did I. My sister didn't come out of the room, and he didn't come back home. I lay down on my tummy, taking advantage because I wasn't allowed to sleep that way. I must have fallen asleep quickly. Nothing seemed to last long; he came back home, and I woke up. I turned around and lay on my back like it was expected of me. I breathe quietly, trying to stay invisible.

I'm thinking about how it will be when we move from this house. We got evicted because my sister hadn't paid the rent. We still have a few days; we should be in the new apartment before the holidays. I love Christmas, even though I'm not expecting any presents. I don't believe in Santa; he brings good toys to the rich and nothing to the poor. I'm not dumb; I know it is the parents who buy the presents. Santa is for kids who have parents.

Oswaldo came to the room and "woke me up." I was awake, but he didn't notice. He took me to the living room and slapped me in the face. You know what God told me? He asked. No, I replied. He said he's tired of you talking to him. I was requested by him to punish you; he is not interested in listening to you. No one loves you besides me, Brenda. Not your mom, not God, only me. Come to the room and meet your punishment. I thought my punishment was going to be sex. To my surprise, there was this German Shepherd dog. He grabbed me by the hair and pushed me into a little closet. He also dragged the dog and locked us both inside.

A new punishment was added to the list.

My sister and her husband are giving me the silent treatment, and I love it. They normally stop talking to me when we are in public. Of all the punishments, this one is the best. I literally get a break from them, especially from my sister's ideas. When they don't talk to me, I am not allowed to eat. Best of all, he won't have sex with me to make me "suffer." For some reason, they both believe that I want to be in a relationship with him and that I enjoy having sex.

I got home from school, and my sister left with her kids, leaving me behind. Four of Oswaldo's friends came to visit, and he played Santeria music for them. They lit a few more candles and incense. He called me into the living room and practically pushed me down on the floor. One of the men said, So, you are the chosen one.

They killed a thin, long snake and a white pigeon. They poured the pigeon's blood into a fancy wine glass in front of the Indian statue and some blood on me while licking their bloody fingers with excitement. I want to run away from them, but I don't dare to move. They are standing side by side, forming a circle around me. One of them grabs the snake and peels off the skin; they all share the freshly raw snake, eating it while they surround me.

I wonder how the real me is doing. Is she still alive? Is she safe in her hiding place? I haven't closed my eyes in a long time. I've been recording nonstop, choosing to be a robot with my eyes open. Maybe I should close them for a moment. I do not wish to record. I must hide! I feel like I can't breathe. I look up, and this man is on top of me. You are a lucky bitch, he whispers. I can't do what I want because he is protecting you. I will not rest until you are unprotected, and then, then you'll see.

Who is guarding me? I wonder. If he couldn't do as he wished, then my protector must be stronger than the Indian or any Santeria god. I must meet him. I have a protector!

Lately I haven't been punished that much. Surprisingly, my sister allowed me to go out with them. It's Saturday, and I don't have to stay behind. We went to McDonald's, and I'm just happy and grateful to be sitting at the table. Today, I am a kid and not a dog!

It's no surprise my sister consistently visits the City Park with her children on sunny days; it's a nice spot. There's a long path to walk on, benches, and a playground shaped like a castle. I love castles; they are strongly built to protect people. I know I'm not supposed to play, so I stand next to the bench where my sister is sitting. The boys are inviting me to play, but I don't dare to move. I can't believe what I'm hearing; Oswaldo is telling me to go and play. I looked at him and smiled. I ran and played with my nephews and my niece. We played on the swings, we played with a ball, and we went down the slides. Then they decided to play hide-and-seek. That's when my brother-in-law joined us. He grabbed me by the hand and told me he would show me a good hiding spot.

He took me into one of the towers of the castle and began to kiss me. Saying, when you smiled at me, I knew you wanted me. A little blonde boy tried to come into the tower, and he just stood there staring at us… The boy didn't say anything. Like everyone else, he turned around and left. I'll bring you back tonight. Go and play, Oswaldo said. I stayed hidden in the tower for a few minutes, feeling ashamed and mad at myself. Why did I smile at him?

Strangely, my sister is in a good mood. She told me I could use the restroom and take a shower. Sometimes, they don't allow me to use the bathroom as a punishment. I thought he had forgotten about the park, but he hadn't. The only reason she let me shower was so her husband could take me out on a date. A quick and spontaneous smile had come at a high price.

He took me back to the park for the first time at night, and we looked like a couple as he held my hand. For some reason, the path felt longer, the park darker and colder. He kept going on and on about his plans. Saying that as soon as I turned eighteen, he would leave my sister. Once again, he took me inside one of the towers to kiss and touch me. It smelled like urine, and it was dark and scary. After a few minutes, he led me to another part of the park. There were stairs, some memorial statues, benches to sit on, and a small pond with a few fish. We weren't the only ones in the park, but I felt alone. There were a few couples nearby, some sitting, others walking holding hands. I guess this place is for kids during the day and for couples at night.

We passed a couple who looked like they were from Central America. One of the men said, Excuse me! Where did you find such a young prostitute? I'll trade you this one and pay you double for her. Oswaldo proudly said, this one is mine! He kept walking, still holding my hand, until we sat on a bench. The man came back more than once, trying to negotiate with cash in his hand, but the answer was still no. According to Oswaldo, I was his girlfriend, and I was not for sale. Whispering, you belong to me, and me only.

The bright place, once warm and full of laughter, had become dark, cold, and silent. A tower built to protect its people had turned into a trap to capture its prisoners. The same park where they spent time with their wives and children during the day was now the secret place where they took their mistresses at night.

There is no difference between a small closet and a big-city park when both become a place for punishment. Every smile costs me something, every breath feels borrowed, and every scream fades into a whisper. Punishment has become a shadow that follows me everywhere I go. It does not matter how fast I run; it still catches up to me. The penalty for doing something wrong, I wonder, what did I do?

Hidden

8

My heart is in anguish within me; the terrors
of death have fallen on me. Fear and trembling
have beset me; horror has overwhelmed me.
I said, Oh, that I had the wings of a dove!
I would fly away and be at rest.
I would flee far away and stay in the desert;
I would hurry to my place of shelter, far from
the tempest and storm.

Psalm 55:4-8 NIV

We moved to a new house. It's bigger and has a backyard, not that it matters to me. It's not like I'm going to enjoy it. What I love about this new place is that it doesn't have roaches, at least not yet. I don't know how long that will last. Lately, I've been thinking about how miserable my life is. Do I really want to turn eighteen and become his wife? How much more can I take? He plans to use me for years and years to come. According to him, this is what my life will look like.

My options are limited. Go back to Puerto Rico with my mother? Stay here and live the rest of my life as their slave? Die? Go to jail? None of them seem easy, but dying would be the least painful. I gave up on dying; nothing I try ever works. Would it make a difference to be punished here or in Puerto Rico? At least here, they're not supposed to love me. My mother was supposed to love me and protect me, and she hasn't. I'm constantly looking for reasons why she doesn't love me or for her to be absent. Why haven't I heard from her? And I can't find one. Maybe staying here with them is my better option. What if I get arrested? If I tell the police, will they arrest me too? I don't know if I can trust them. After all, James is a corrupt cop who buys drugs and hits his wife.

Emilia rents a mailbox at the post office, Box 1553. There's a plaza nearby, and that's where they usually stop for fast food. I walked into a store and stole a fancy pencil. My plan to get caught worked. A tall, blond man took me to the back of the store and called the police. When they arrived, they asked for my sister's information and not a single question about me. Soon after, Oswaldo came and talked to the officers, and just like that, I was back in his hands. Surprisingly, he was happy. He even stopped to celebrate at the Chinese restaurant. He said I was finally becoming a bad girl. My plan failed.

It's winter now, so my sister doesn't go out as much. He can't take me to the park at night because it is cold, and it gets dark early in the evening. Occasionally, he asks his brother Will to let him use his apartment instead. When he does, he turns into an animal. As soon as Will hands him the keys, he throws me on the living room floor and quickly has sex with me. I can't shower at Will's place, but it doesn't matter. There's no point in showering when I can't clean myself.

I don't like Will. He opens the door to his apartment, looks at me with a mix of pity and disgust, and then walks away. I hate the way people look at me. Like I'm something filthy just because I am my sister's lover's girlfriend. As if it were my choice and not theirs. People look at me like they're shopping, like I'm a discounted item on a shelf. They grab me, scan me, and bet a price. A bag of food or a loan of ten to twenty dollars. A few pills or diapers.

The family keeps the dirty laundry hidden. Friends mind their own business, and neighbors don't snitch. While teachers are out for a salary. I am surrounded by people who are too busy protecting themselves. No one listens, no one speaks, no one sees, or they pretend not to. Those are the same people who cry during movies, who gasp at news reports about abuse, and then ask how no one saw or said anything. The truth is that, just like me, they're scared. I'm realizing now that it takes more than a voice to speak up. It takes courage. Maybe one day I'll find the strength to speak.

After all,… It's their secret, not mine. The men with prostitutes. The police officer, his brother, and his friends. My mother, my sisters, and their husbands. They're the weak ones. It seems to me that, just like me, they are guilty, yet I am the only one being punished.

Christmas is around the corner, and my sister is going out shopping. I'm not allowed to ask for presents because I'm not their daughter, but I'm not sad; I already know Santa isn't real. My nephew's birthday is also on Christmas Day, and they're planning a big party. Today, they bought me a pair of jean overalls. They were on sale since they're a summer style with shorts, and because it's winter, no one wants to buy them. But I'm happy—this is the first time I've been given brand-new clothing that wasn't passed down or stained. While we were at the store, I saw this stuffed animal that looked like a real dog. Oswaldo noticed me staring at it and asked if I wanted it. He said that since I'm his girlfriend, he might get it for me as a gift.

We stopped by a fast-food place with a playground. I was allowed to go inside and play because they met with some neighbors and friends. I played with a boy in the ball pit. It was the first time we'd ever talked, even though we went to the same school. I laughed genuinely. Oswaldo saw me laughing and playing, and he got mad. He came over and ordered me to get out. Just like that, I wasn't allowed to play anymore. I stepped out of the playground and stood on the side, watching the other kids from a distance. My freedom was cut short, but I enjoyed it while it lasted.

They kept talking to their friends, and I quietly slipped away to use the bathroom without asking for permission. When I came out of the restroom, Oswaldo was waiting right outside the door. Wait until we get home, he warned me. I knew what that meant. From that moment the punishment with the silent treatment began. I stood like a soldier, next to them almost becoming invisible to society as if I possessed a superpower of invisibility.

At home, they didn't speak to me. I knew I had to go sit next to the dog in the dark corner, which I did. That's where I go when I'm being punished. I was punishing myself when Oswaldo opened the closet door. You like to go pee, huh? He asked as he started to urinate on me as part of my punishment. Now, I'm not allowed to use the bathroom, and if I do, he says I'll have to drink his urine. When he was done, he closed the closet door. As I sat there, soaked in the dark, next to the dog. I covered my mouth to giggle. It doesn't matter how humiliating the punishment is; if they don't see me cry, I win. Today was worth it. I played and laughed, and I used the bathroom. When I was done using the toilet, I washed my hands and face. I drank water from the sink. I did all of that with the adrenaline rushing me to hurry. I did it, and it was all worth it. Today I won.

I always go to the restroom when I'm at school, but since we're on Christmas vacation, I must hold it until I'm given permission. The day of the party is finally here, and they're in a good mood. Oswaldo told me I was allowed to eat today. I'm not a big eater; food usually makes me sick to my stomach, but today I'm trying some new things that other people made. My sister even took a picture of me with her kids. She asked me to smile and look happy because she was going to send it to our mother. So, I tried to look happy. Sometimes I get confused, not knowing when to smile or if it's okay to cry. I can't tell when the right moment is. My emotions don't belong to me anymore; they belong to them. They own everything about me.

Loud music is playing, and people are dancing, eating, drinking, and using drugs. I'm trying to enjoy it as much as I can because I know I'll have to pay for it later. I also really need to use the bathroom, but I'm not allowed to ask when there are people around.

Maybe they won't notice if I sneak away; they seem distracted. Should I take a chance? Will he pee in my mouth if he catches me? I can't hold it any longer. Just like at the fast-food restaurant, he was waiting for me when I came out. He grabbed me by the hand and took me to his bedroom. He slapped me and told me to stay in the room until I was done crying.

I wiped my face dry as fast as I could and went back outside to play. But I stopped after a few minutes. Something didn't feel right. I was feeling guilty for having fun, like I was disobeying them. Perhaps I really do deserve all the punishments and to be treated like a dog because I act like one. I'm wearing a brand-new outfit. I was allowed to eat as much as I wanted. I got to run and talk to people and laugh. Still, I couldn't obey the rules. I always manage to do something wrong. They gave me a little freedom, and it feels bad. It's overwhelming. I don't know what to do with it. I feel out of place. I can't wait for the party to be over. I want to go into the closet. They are no longer the problem. I am, and the guilty feeling proves it.

It's Christmas Day, and the kids are opening their presents. I've been cleaning up the mess from last night's party. Bottles, cups, and food all over the place. While they're distracted with their new toys, I sneak some scraps to the dog from the leftover plates. I don't give him bones, though. I don't want his gums to get swollen like mine.

Oswaldo comes over and tells me to hurry because he has a surprise for me. Instead, I do the opposite by taking my time. I don't trust him, and I don't like his surprises.

A few minutes later, he comes back and tells me I can play the new video game he got for himself. I shouldn't believe him, but I do. I still have to finish the dishes, though. I heard his brother Rolando is coming over to visit the boys today, so now I'm trying to hurry. I like it when Rolando comes. He smiles at me, and when I get punished, he quietly tells me it'll be okay. Sometimes just hearing those words helps. I head over to the dog's closet. I need to clean it and make sure he ate all the food I gave him earlier. He did. I quickly clean everything up just in case I get punished later in the day.

Out of nowhere, Oswaldo comes and gives me the stuffed animal, the one I saw at the store. He says it's a Christmas present. For a second, I believed in the magic of Christmas. But then he asks me if I really want it. He says if I decide to keep it, I'll have to have sex with him, and that will be the returned gift from me to him. For the first time he is giving me a choice, and somehow that makes me feel grateful. Aside from feeling that he is doing something nice for me by giving me the chance to decide. I'm thinking if I do stay with the gift, it'll be the only object in this house that belongs to me. So, I chose to keep it. It's the first time I've made a trade for something that is just for me and not for someone else. It doesn't feel good, but he is going to have sex with me anyway, right? At least this way, I'll have something that is mine. A stuffed animal like those girls on the TV have, and that will make me feel like a normal girl for once.

Emilia is furious because he gave me a gift. She tells me I deserve nothing but a box full of excrement. I try to ignore her; the same way Oswaldo is ignoring her. For some reason it feels like today he is on my side, and I won't let her ruin it with her words. Today I want to be a regular kid on Christmas day.

My sister has an appointment today. She goes to talk to a therapist. She says she needs someone to know about me, just in case I ever talk and get her in trouble. According to her, she's already covered. Her therapist knows she's the victim, and I'm the bad sister who stole her man. She laughs about it, saying she should've been an actress because she can cry on demand, and her therapist believes every word. She tells me how the therapist feels sorry for her.

I wonder if people that are supposed to help can really tell when someone is lying. Can they see who's mean underneath the tears, or do they just sit and listen because that's what they get paid to do? I want to be a therapist when I grow up. Maybe I'll learn how to see through fake crying. I'll be the kind of person who knows when someone like me is telling the truth or, like my sister, is lying.

While she's out at her appointment, Oswaldo tells me it's time to pay for the gift I kept. I wish I had never taken it. Why do I always make the wrong choices? I don't understand why I always have to pay. They get money from the government. I clean the house, help with the drugs, keep watch for the police, and run errands. No one pays me for that; I do it all for free. Why do I have to pay for something that was given to me as a gift?

He says I have to please him. I have to kiss him and pretend to desire him. I still don't know how to do any of that. It still hurts, I still cry, and my body trembles. I told him I do not want to have sex, but he didn't care. When he was done with me, he threw the stuffed animal in the trash because I did not please him. He looked at me and said, I will show you what happens when people don't pay back what they owe me.

My sister leaves the house whenever drugs are being prepared. She doesn't want to get caught if the police do a raid. That way, she can claim she didn't know anything. She always has some kind of escape plan, an alibi ready, and a performance rehearsed. Staying just far enough from the mess to avoid blame. Unlike me.

I assume he's going to have sex with me when she's gone. That's how it usually goes. But this time, something feels off. He hasn't asked me to shower. Maybe he's expecting someone; there are always people calling him and stopping by to buy drugs. He keeps pacing, glancing at the clock, and I just sit here, waiting for him to drag me to hell again. It feels strange not knowing what to expect. I'm used to the routine, to the cycle that never breaks. So, I do what I've learned to do best: breathe quietly. I don't speak, and I barely move while I make myself invisible. There's a knock at the door. Oswaldo orders me to hide under the stairs outside in the hallway and to stay still. Watch everything, he says. I do as I'm told. It's a drug deal, a quick exchange of money and product.

He comes back inside but won't stop pacing. Then there is another knock. Again, he hides me under the stairs and says, Watch everything. This time, he invites the customer into the hallway, then grabs a bat he had stashed under the stairs. With no warning, he swings. The man collapses, and Oswaldo drags him closer to me. He hits him again and again. With the bat, his fists, and his feet. The man begs for him to stop, but Oswaldo doesn't listen. This is what happens when people don't pay their debts, he says. He stares at me as he utters those words. He kept hitting the man, not because of drugs, but to deliver me a message. I kept the gift and didn't pay for it like I was supposed to. It was never a gift. I bought it on credit.

How can one person hold so much power over another? I sometimes wonder, maybe he is the one with evil intentions and my sister is the victim, like the role she plays. Or could it be she is the evil one? Why does she allow this? How can she enjoy it? Is this really going to be my life forever? The truth is, they are both villains. They are both guilty. Still, I carry the weight of shame for things I haven't done. If I'm not the one doing wrong, why am I always the one being punished? Why does no one stand up for me? When will that day come, and who will that person be? What can I possibly do to redeem myself? When will this end? Can someone save me?

I'm scared that one day he will beat me the same way he beat that man under the stairs. I still don't understand why men who are supposed to be stronger than girls don't fight back. I wish I had the strength of a man. I'm sure I could push him off. But I'm just a girl, so I must obey. I need to stop running through the clouds looking for a castle that doesn't exist. He always gets mad when I freeze. I look like a motionless doll, blank, unable to satisfy him. He says I'm no different from a piece of furniture, and if I don't start acting like a woman, he'll keep treating me like a dog. He told me one day we'll be stuck together like dogs in heat.

I hate the way he looks at me and licks his lips like a serpent. His sweat, his weight pressing into me, the smell of him. That's why I'll keep running through the clouds. It's the only place left where I can survive this nightmare. I know they want to break me until there's nothing left, but I will not die by their hands. The Indian's thirst will not be satisfied by my blood. I will survive and become stronger than them both. Even if I have to stay hidden in the closet.

Do As You Wish

9

For it is shameful even to speak
of the things that they do in secret.

Ephesians 5:12 ESV

Spring is here, and it feels like there's a battle between the hot and cold temperatures. It's fascinating to watch the trees resurrect themselves; in the blink of an eye, they've come alive again. Just yesterday they slept beneath a snow-white blanket, and now, as if summoned, they must get dressed for the upcoming summer. I also must get ready. With summer comes my birthday, which opened a sinkhole last year that dragged me into hell. Almost one year later, and I'm still waiting to be rescued.

With the warmer weather, my sister goes out more, which means I spend more Saturdays with him. We also take more walks to the park, the same park that during the day plays songs of laughter for the children but drowns me in sorrow and terror at night. Two places in one. It gives life to some and takes it away from others. Oh, how I hate this park! I see couples walking by and wonder if they are in love or is she being dragged. When a man gives a gift, is it out of love, or is it payment for something he plans to take? The one thing that makes one person happy can break another person's heart. A reward for one can be punishment for the other.

The closet is supposed to be my punishment, but today, it isn't. It's my sanctuary. A dark little place where no one sees if I cry or smile. Even though the floor is covered in pee and filth, I can finally breathe. I don't have to be invisible. No one talks in here; no one listens. I'm in the closet today because I used the toilet when he allowed me to shower. I've been sitting on this wet, sticky floor, and what disgusts me the most is knowing his white glue is still inside me. Out of all the corners in this house, this is my favorite. I could pee in the tub and avoid punishment, but instead, I chose the toilet, hoping they'll send me here. I know it won't take long before they figure it out, but for now, I'll enjoy this small space.

My sister was talking on the phone when Oswaldo took me into his bedroom. He leans in and whispers, we are going to let you talk to your mom. Don't you dare to say anything about us. I'll be listening on the other phone. My mom? Do I even have a mother? Since I got on that plane, I haven't heard from her. I picked up the phone, and Emilia stays right by my side. I can see Oswaldo across the hallway, holding the other phone, listening to the conversation.

My mother tells me I have a new sister. Daughter number nine. I stay quiet. Are you happy? She asks. Oswaldo frantically shakes his head yes, so I say yes. But all I can think of is, another baby? I'm glad I left that house. Just hearing her voice makes me feel uncomfortable. She's describing how beautiful the baby is: with black curly hair, light skin, and green eyes. Aren't you going to ask what her name is? She presses. What's the baby's name? I ask. She tells me she has a surprise: we're coming to the United States; we will all be together again. When the call ends, I ask myself, am I happy? Because honestly, I am not. She didn't even tell me the baby's name.

Oswaldo pulls me aside every day. Promise you won't leave. I love you. I swear I'll leave your sister when you turn eighteen. Your mom hates you; she doesn't want you to be happy. To then build an imaginary future. Reassuring that everything bad he does to me is my sister's fault. Without her, there would be no punishments.

My sister is furious. She either insults me or hits me every time she sees me. You're happy she's coming, aren't you? You can't wait to leave me. You want me to get sick with HIV. You ungrateful whore. Each word comes with a slap, a shove, or a fistful of hair.

Emilia has been obsessing over how things will play out when Mom arrives. Out of nowhere, she comes up with this brilliant plan: Oswaldo can provoke our brother into a crisis so that he gets locked up in a psychiatric hospital. As for Mom, she says getting rid of her will be easy. All they have to do is get her drunk. Then Emilia will provoke her and call the police to claim she's an alcoholic and abusive. That way, she can try to get custody of our little sister. She even jokes that her husband will need to have sex with Mom, because that's what she does when she is drunk.

Emilia laughs and says that since I haven't been able to please her husband, he should move on to Leilani. She thinks Tanairí is too old and probably not a virgin, so the next one in line should be Leilani. According to her, becoming a legal guardian is simple, just like they did with me. The more she talks; the more Oswaldo seems to like the idea. And that makes her even more excited. She skips around the house, laughing like it's some type of game and she's winning.

The punishments have slowed down. He still has sex with me, but it feels like he has accepted that I'll never be able to please him the way he wants. Sometimes he tells me he loves me, that he'll prove it to me. He even argues with Emilia when she asks him to punish me. He refuses, as if he's protecting me. But then, he turns cold again. You're worthless. No one will ever love you. You're just a whore. Then his tone shifts: I'm the only one who loves you. As soon as you turn eighteen, I'll treat you like a real wife. He says he worries about me. If anyone finds out we're together, they'll send us both to jail. I'm strong; I can fight. But you? You'd never survive. They'll eat you alive. Everyone will hate you for betraying your sister.

I've been thinking that I don't want him to do the same thing to Leilani. I promised I would protect her. This is all my fault because I don't know how to please a man. I'm almost eleven years old and still haven't learned. If something ever happens to her because of me, I'll never forgive myself. I refuse to follow in the footsteps of others and turn my back on her. She still has a chance at life. That night, I waited until everyone was asleep and quietly cried myself to sleep.

In the morning, the sadness didn't go away. No matter how much I think about it, I'm not smart enough to come up with a solution. I'm afraid I'll give up without even putting up a fight. I'm a coward just like them. Emilia saw me crying and asked why. I told her I didn't want Oswaldo to be with Leilani. She burst out laughing. Like, it was funny. Announcing to her husband, "Brenda is jealous!" But I wasn't jealous; I was scared and now misunderstood. I didn't want my little sister to hurt like me. So, I became the joke of the day, and I didn't dare to defend myself. I was too ashamed. Too afraid to lift my voice and explain myself.

I hate her for being so heartless. It disgusts me how proud she is of choosing who her husband should cheat with. She doesn't care if it's her sister or even her mother, as long as she's the one in control. She doesn't care if he sells drugs or beats someone. As long as she gets her allowance and her mouth stays full. She decides who has sex with him. She tells him when I cry or smile. She owns me; it's all her fault.

God… if you're really the one protecting me, then please, help me. You must rescue me, or I won't survive. Please, God!

A few days ago, I told them I would do anything they wanted only if they promised to leave Leilani out of this sick relationship. I cried and begged until they accepted my offer. As part of the deal, I will live with them forever. I will obey them to protect my sister. Today, Emilia left with the kids to visit a friend. Before walking out the door, she reminded me not to forget our deal. As soon as they were gone, I cleaned the table and began setting up the materials. I was getting ready to be on the lookout when Oswaldo ordered me to go into the bedroom instead. He turned on a pornographic movie and ordered me to sit on the bed and watch it while he prepared the drugs.

I don't like seeing naked people. It scares me to watch someone else get hurt like me. But I had to keep my eyes open. I felt a wave of shame as I stared at the screen. Like I was the one doing something wrong or my body was being exposed. Understanding now why my sister and stepdad say I'm ugly. The women in those movies have nice hair. Their skin looks smooth, with no hair on their armpits. Emilia says if I want to get rid of the hair under my arms, I have to let her rip each one out with a tweezer. That hurts too much.

After a while, Oswaldo came in and asked what I had learned from the movie. I didn't answer. I hadn't learned anything. He asked if I had watched it, and I said yes. I watched it but didn't remember any details. So, he rewound the movie and played it from the start. Telling me to pay attention. I tried, but my mind kept wandering off. What if the police raid the house? Would they arrest me because of the porn movie? Are the people in the movie being forced?

He comes back into the room and asks if I paid attention. I say yes, hoping he wouldn't ask anything else. I really did try to pay attention.

Wanting to count the tiles on the ceiling, I kept miscounting, and then I ended up forgetting both the tiles and the movie.

He started to have sex with me and got mad because I couldn't please him. Again, he played the movie from the beginning and told me to watch it while he went to shower. When he returned, he tried to have sex with me, and once more, I failed. He couldn't finish. So again, he rewound the movie and left me watching it. I would rather not learn anything from it. He comes back and says, if you don't want me to replace you with your sister, then prove to me that you're worth it. I want you to be exactly like that whore from the movie. This is your last chance, do you understand?

I look at the screen, and all I feel is hopelessness. There's no way I can be like her. He gives me the chance anyway, and I fail. He still hasn't finished. I don't excite him like the woman in the movie does. I cry and cry because I can't save my sister. He goes into the kitchen to get something to eat. I stayed in the bedroom, still watching the movie, alone. Why doesn't he get tired? I'm exhausted. I feel filthy and just want to shower, but I haven't been given permission. I'm not just failing him; I'm failing in my promise to protect Leilani.

While he eats in the kitchen, I sit naked on the bed, crying and feeling defeated. I was supposed to be on the lookout for police, and now I can't even lift my head. I must breathe quietly; maybe if I'm still enough, he'll forget about me. I can't cry or move, and I can't think. I need to disappear. I must stop existing; I want to die. I think he forgot about me after he ate. He sat in the living room to watch television, and I stayed on the bed, paralyzed. I'm so tired of being in the same position, but I don't dare to move.

Every time there's a loud noise from the TV, I take advantage of it to breathe deeply before returning to being invisible. I wonder if this is how it feels to be dead, to lie motionless and breathless for eternity. I get scared and bite the inside of my cheek just to make sure I'm still alive. I won't die as long as I'm not lying on my back. That's the position for sex, for nightmares, and for the dead to sleep in.

In school, we learned about the stars. I found out the sun is just one giant star. All this time, I thought I knew where God was hiding, but He wasn't even there. I still haven't told anyone the secret of his hiding place. I feel abandoned by him. I wish I could pray, but I'm convinced God gets mad at me for speaking. That's why I barely talk anymore, not because I'm shy. My mouth was shut by others.

There's a girl a year older than me, and sometimes we walk together to school. Her stepdad is a friend of my brother-in-law and one of the men who ate the snake. One morning, she was crying and told me she couldn't take it anymore. She asked me to come with her so we could both talk about what they do to us. She believes we can be saved, that they might put us in the same home. I told her it was better to stay quiet, that no one would care. But she still went ahead and talked in school. A few weeks later, she was punished by her stepdad. He introduced a broomstick inside her vagina, and she ended up in the hospital. It came on the news, and that's when the teachers finally believed her. By then, it was too late. People don't believe horror stories unless they come out on TV. Most are afraid of becoming the voice for someone who can't speak.

Oswaldo finished watching TV and is now listening to music. I wish I could take a shower, just to sneak a few sips of water.

I don't drink much anymore because if I have to use the bathroom and I don't get permission, it hurts to hold it in. And if I do get permission, I must wait until they inspect the toilet before I'm allowed to flush so he can make sure I only peed.

Oh no… that song again. It's one of the new ones that talks about sex. Every time it comes on the radio, my brother-in-law says they wrote it for me because that's the only thing men want from me. To prove it, he made me sit and listen to it over and over until I wrote the lyrics perfectly, without mistakes. He always says, every guy knows you're a whore. When they look at you, that's what they think about having sex with you. You're a sex doll.

I also believe that's how they all see me, as a sex slave. All these monsters are drawn to me like I've been marked with a hot branding iron. It's an invisible brand only they can see. No one has ever said I'm special, good, or worthy of love. They only point out my flaws. They decide who I am: another broken girl destined to be a whore that no one will ever love.

That song, the one people sing and dance to, he always smiles and stares at me when it plays. The lyrics describe being alone with her, undressing her, and touching her while telling her to be quiet. That's what he does to me. That's the scene every time my sister leaves me behind, and that's what happens when he takes me to the bathroom at night. The same thing happens at Will's apartment, right after he gets the keys. A song that makes someone else happy and becomes a party anthem became my nightmare. A catchy beat that haunts me. The song reminded him that I was waiting for him, naked. He came back and asked, did you watch the movie? Yes, I said.

He asks, did you learn from her? Yes, I learned. Well, what are you waiting for? I tried, but I couldn't control my trembling body. I didn't know what to do. My mind wanted to run away, but I had to stay present to prove myself. It's difficult to please him like the woman in the porn movie. I don't know how to do something that hurts this much.

Back when I lived in Puerto Rico, my sister Mara used to meet with an old man in San Juan. He would take her to a house and film her with these expensive cameras while she got naked. He paid her, and she liked it. She would have sex with him just like a porn actress. The first time she took me with her, I got so sick and threw up. I went back home alone, sick to my stomach.

Tears ran down my cheeks, and before he could get mad at me for crying, I told him it was because I was tired and thirsty. I begged him, If I drink something, I'll be able to do it. Please, allow me to have a drink. I wanted one little sip of water; that's all I was hoping for.

Okay, he said. He stood up, walked to the kitchen, and came back with a glass of water. Lie down on your back and open your mouth. I'll give you something to drink. I quickly obeyed, and he got too close. He smirked, like he always does when he enjoys himself. Getting face-to-face with me, he began spitting into my mouth. I tried to move, but he grabbed me hard. I couldn't escape.

This is what I want you to drink, he said. You make me do things no one else does. You drive me crazy. It's your fault I'm doing this. This is what you want; you make me do this. This is your fault. Are you still thirsty? He asked. Tell me when to stop. Tell me you're satisfied. Stop, I told him. I'm not thirsty anymore. Please! I'm not thirsty.

Do I want him to do this? Is this what I was hoping to drink? No, but this is what he's giving me. It's disgusting. He's drooling all over my face like a dog with rabies, repeating over and over, it's your fault; this is what you asked for. I can smell his saliva and sweat. My stomach churns, but I have no choice but to keep swallowing.

He asks, did I satisfy your thirst? Yes, I reply. Come and do as she do, he says while he lies down on the bed. Insisting for me to hurry. The woman in the movie is on top of the man. I'm trapped in a hole to avoid doing this. There's no turning back. I take a deep breath and lie on top of him. Put it in, he says. What are you waiting for?

I jump off in panic and stand on the floor. I look at my body and burst into tears. My heart is about to run away from my chest, and my mind is about to crash. How is it possible for time to travel at the speed of light while it is standing still? I don't think my mind can take so much confusion, nor can my eyes record so much horror.

I have nothing to put inside of you. What do you want me to put in?

He grabs me by the hair. You just want to get me more excited, don't you? He growls. Put it inside of you. Today you will be pregnant.

You're driving me crazy. I can't wait for you to be done, and when you are, don't get off too quickly. We're going to get stuck like dogs. I'll be stuck inside of you, and if you get off too fast, all your insides will come out and you'll die. Look at you. This is what you wanted. You made me do this. It's your fault.

I stare at the TV and mimic the actress. I do what he expects from me. I lie and tell him I like it, even though I feel disgustingly sick. I can't wait for the movie to end. Meanwhile, he is enjoying every second. For the first time, our roles are reversed. I'm the one on top, still, I'm the one in pain. Trembling with fear.

Lucky for me, he's finally done using me. He tells me to get off because he's done. I started crying again. I'm constantly trying to push him off, but not today. I'm doing the opposite; holding on to him with my dear life. Oh, you liked it, he says, smiling. Get off; I'm done with you. I say no, and he laughs. Do you want more? He asks.

I stay quiet. The truth is that I am terrified of being stuck like the dogs; I know any movement will be painful for me. Slowly, I stand up, placing my hand in between my legs. I'm afraid that my insides will fall out. Maybe if I hold them in, I can push them back inside. He gives me permission to shower. I know I should get dressed first, but I stay naked and run for the shower. I feel sick to my stomach. I need to make sure my insides do not come out of me.

"Terror" isn't even the right word for what I am feeling. Please, God, don't let my insides come out. Please!

As I step out of the bedroom, my sister is standing there. Slapping me across the face, she says, "I trusted you with my husband, and this is what you do? Her words stab my heart. My knees buckle, and I fall. I did what they asked me to do. I feel so guilty, and I ask her to forgive me. This time I was the one on top, and she saw me. I can't control the guilty feeling that is overtaking me. It's my fault. Oswaldo comes out and tells me to go shower before the kids see me naked.

As soon as I get into the shower, I throw up. My stomach still hurts. I need to use the bathroom, but he hasn't given me permission. I can't hold it anymore. Shame on me, I had diarrhea in the shower. Luckily, he didn't come to check on me. So, I got away with it.

 When I come out, he sends me to sit in the closet with the dog. This time, I believe I deserve it. On my way to the closet, he stops me and hands me a piece of cake with a lit candle. My nephew says, Happy Birthday, Brenda! As he goes back to his games. While Oswaldo was closing the closet door, he said, Today was special, but you must be punished. Your sister said so. Happy Birthday!

I sat in the closet next to the dog, holding my guilt like a gift I never asked for. Today they did as they wished, as they always do. I was so exhausted that, in the darkness of the closet, I ate my piece of cake. On another occasion, I would have given it to the dog, but this time, whether out of anger or survival, I ate it.

Each bite will echo. It's my fault! It's my fault! Just like my mother, I forgot that today was my birthday. I'm eleven years old, and I'm celebrating it alone, in a closet. It's my fault! It's my fault!

For Their Own Good

10

What sorrow awaits you who lie awake at night,
Thinking up evil plans. You rise at dawn,
and hurry to carry them out, simply because
you have the power to do so.
Micah 2:1 NLT

My sister is convinced that I had sex with the intention to destroy her relationship. She acts like it's a competition, and he is some great trophy that everyone wants to win. I told her I was following orders, which she arranged as part of the deal, but she wouldn't hear it. She's still angry, claiming she feels betrayed. I feel confused. How can she feel betrayed when it was all her idea? She's the one making the deals, deciding who, when, and where. The truth is, she wants me to feel guilty so she can have her story straight in case anything ever comes out. It's all about control. She plays mind games, plans evil, and plays her victim role while others carry out her dirty work.

I'm growing tired of her. I know the deal is that I'm supposed to stay with them, but I can't keep that promise. I will play her game until my little sister is safe and far away. Then I'll escape, even if I die trying. I'll get away from all of them. Until then, every time she plays the victim, I apologize. That's what keeps her satisfied. I can see the smirk on her face and how her whole mood shifts like a flipped switch when she feels in control again.

Emilia says the day I walk out that door, I'll end up in a psych ward. If I ever talk, no one will believe me; they'll think I'm crazy. I'm beginning to think she's the one who belongs in a psychiatric hospital. I don't have to be an adult or a therapist to see that her wickedness is eating her alive. I wonder if she even sleeps at night. She wakes up bursting with ideas, excited to carry them out like missions. Lights up when she orders her husband to have sex with me or the Christian single mom who lives next door. It's mind-blowing how much she enjoys it. Her mood depends on wickedness.

I barely get punished, mostly because my sister forgave me for what I did. There's a new rule: only he can have sex with me, not the other way around. He's only allowed to use me when she's in her period, when she's tired, or not in the mood, but that's nothing new. I'm the second option, and I shouldn't be the one asking for sex. She told me she didn't mind when he was dating Mara, but then Mara started wanting more attention. Since she is the mother of his two sons, she has priority. If I want more privileges, then I need to have a baby.

They say they're trying to change to prove how much they love me, or so they claim. They want me to stay when my mother comes from Puerto Rico. Emilia says our mother has plans to take me to another state. She's afraid of me leaving; that means he will get another girlfriend, and she won't be from the family. She will lose control.

Lately, she's been doing good things for me. Allowing me to shower when I smell, letting me use the shampoo and the big comb to detangle my curly hair. I can use the toilet and flush without them checking once a day. She gives me two or three menstrual pads instead of just one. I'm allowed to have one cup a day of whatever drink I choose. She even promised that one day, after Mom leaves, she'll take me to eat breakfast with them. That'll be my reward if I stay.

I've become her favorite sister, and she says she's happy I'm living with her because she doesn't feel lonely anymore. Today was a good day. Once a day feels like a luxury compared to none. But I know she's pretending; her kindness is fear in disguise. She's scared I might talk. She's not afraid of me going to jail; she's terrified that he will. The idea of losing him will mean the end of the world for her.

I've been keeping my word, trying to behave more like his girlfriend. I don't like making excuses after giving my word. Mom used to lie all the time. She'd say, I promise I'll buy you a toy if you come to the store with me. Then when the day came, she'd say, I'm broke; I'll get it for you next month. Once, I made her promise to buy me a dolly. I didn't tell her why I wanted it. It was right before my birthday, and I knew she'd forget. I behaved my best that July. Keeping my brother happy, and for the whole month, there were no tantrums. There was peace at home, thanks to my sacrifices.

On August third, my brother woke up early, impatient to go out. I was excited too, but I kept calm. We went to the stores. She bought diapers, medicine, and a few supplies. Then we went to this expensive clothing store, and she bought my brother a suit. At the bus terminal, as we were heading home, I reminded her about the plastic imitation doll she had promised me. She said she didn't have any money left. I told her it was only two dollars. She had spent over a hundred on my brother's suit. She must've had something left. But she still said no. She had used my money from my father's check to buy his suit. I was mad and called her a liar, and she slapped me.

I will always find a way to keep my promises. When Oswaldo tells me to do something, I do it. I won't give him a reason to look at my little sister. I'll protect her, no matter what the cost. I just need to stop running away in my mind. That's my biggest weakness, the one thing that always gets me into trouble, and I can't control it. If I could just disappear in my mind while still physically obeying him, I'd be the perfect girlfriend. Even if I'm only pretending, like my sister does. But I'm not a good actress. He does not feel pleased with me.

My mother and siblings arrived in the United States, and it feels strange being around them again. Mom shares a bedroom with all my sisters. Emilia stayed with her husband. One room for her kids, and my brother was given the attic. He's not the favorite one here, but Emilia has a plan, and it's better for him to be isolated. She and Oswaldo had tried everything to provoke him, but it didn't work. Maybe he's older now, and that's why he doesn't throw tantrums like before. Perhaps I was the reason all along. Was it really my fault, like they always said? His outbursts were because of me.

I feel like I'm being pulled between both sides of the family. My mother wants me to stay in her bedroom, and so does Emilia. Mom keeps asking, are you coming with us to Boston? Her voice changes when she wants to sound sweet, and I hate that. Do they really want me with them? I wish there were another option, because I don't want to be with either of them. It feels like the decision has been dumped on me, and they're all playing a game they're afraid of losing.

Now that the house is full, Oswaldo can't have sex with me as often as he wants. But his brother Will keeps giving him the keys to his apartment so he can take me there. Oswaldo talks about how much he'll miss me if my mom manages to take me away. He says all we have to do is wait a few more years until I turn eighteen.

I'm not being punished anymore, and I don't understand why. The dog seems to have a bigger space now that he is locked in the basement. I envy the dog; I miss the silence in the closet. I hate how they keep repeating the same things over and over. I can't breathe. So, I go and hide in a closet, where I can finally breathe again. I punish myself voluntarily, and no one notices.

I went out with Oswaldo to do a drug delivery, and he is telling me that my mom is mad because she wants to have sex with him, and he told her no. He says that he will keep his part of the deal; he won't be with anyone else besides Emilia and me. My mother is angry, so he is concerned about me. He thinks she intends to take me to Boston and then put me in jail for betraying my sister. He says since I am a minor, they can give me fifteen years in prison for what I did in the box. I tell him I'm not worried about it; I'm not telling her anything.

He says, your mother knows we're together. Your sister wanted revenge, and your mom knows it. Because of you, Emilia didn't grow up with her dad; besides, one of your uncles touched her. Why do you think everyone hates you? Your mom knows I'm not interested in being with her. She even asked if I was in a relationship with you. She's furious, I rejected her for you. Come on, you know how your mother is. If you go with her to Boston, she won't be able to punish you or beat you like she did in Puerto Rico, but she will send you to jail. Then, to avoid being arrested, you will need to flee. If that happens, don't come back. You lose everything the moment you choose to leave me. Here, I protect you, and no one else has touched you. Your mom never protected you, and she never will.

He continues, In Puerto Rico, we did an assault at a gas station. A man tried to be a hero, holding on to his wallet. I shot him, and you know how much money he had? Fourteen dollars. He died over fourteen dollars. Since they caught one of the guys, I had to move here. Are you ready to run from the police? Are you willing to kill for money? Where will you even go? You'll have to prostitute yourself because that's the only thing, you're good at. Think about it. With me, you won't have to do any of that. I won't let anyone touch you.

Later in the afternoon, my mom decides to take my siblings to the park, and she invites me. I don't know what to say. I'm not allowed to go out for fun. What time is it? Soon it will be full of couples and no children. Will I get punished if I accept? In the blink of an eye, we're already there. I must have turned into a robot and followed her instructions. It's the same park he takes me to at night. I don't like this park, but it seems to be the one everyone else enjoys.

It's a little chilly; we're in the middle of fall, and there's a colorful blanket of leaves covering the ground. My little sisters run towards the playground, laughing and chasing each other around the castle. They're amazed by squirrels leaping from one tree to another. I found an empty bench nearby and sit down to watch. My mother sits next to me and starts asking questions: What's going on between you and Oswaldo? Nothing, I reply. But she keeps pressing. I know there's something between you two. Tell me I won't say anything.

So, my brother-in-law was telling the truth. She knows. But instead of feeling safe, I feel afraid. Why are you asking me if you already know? I feel betrayed. Why aren't you standing up for me? I feel abandoned; you left me here. I am eleven years old, and you are asking me to talk to you about a relationship. I know it is simply wrong. The whole conversation is happening in my head. Now I'm always quiet, she should be proud of me; I barely talk.

She keeps asking questions, but I stopped listening. I'm trying to listen to the silence. I don't like people talking to me. She wants me to move with them to Boston, and I wonder, what for? Will my life be any better with her? Does she need someone to run errands?

What's going on? My mother is arguing with Emilia and Oswaldo over a phone call. While my sisters gather all their belongings as fast as they can. My mother practically drags me outside after grabbing my hand. Emilia is asking me to stay, and Oswaldo is giving me a death stare. I don't know what to do. I don't want to go to Boston.

It's a rainy night. My sisters and I are getting soaked, standing in the middle of the street. They're still arguing while Mom tries to gather her things. I can't hear them clearly, and I'm not trying to. The sound of the rain is soothing. I focus on the way each drop ends its journey on the ground, only to begin another in a puddle. Wondering how many hidden animals will come out for a sip, like the ones I take when no one's watching. The rain washes the dirt off the streets, leaving the park empty. It scares the bad people away. Everyone hides inside; no one likes to get wet. Except for me, I love the rain. Tears slid down my cheeks, and no one knows I'm crying. I feel free, but not safe. I can cry and smile at the same time because no one notices. The rain hides my emotions, blurs them away.

We walked through the storm, searching for a pay phone. When she finds one, my mom calls her family from Boston. We still have to wait for her nephew to pick us up and drive us to Massachusetts. Why did she even ask if I wanted to go with her when she had already made the choice? A woman comes out of nowhere and invites us to spend the night at her place. A stranger who is kind enough to open her doors. I lay down on the living room floor because that is what I am supposed to do at a stranger's house. The lady was kind. She gave us towels and blankets to warm up. I hear my mother telling her she didn't expect them to abuse me.

I can't believe I'm leaving Pennsylvania, the place I called home for almost two years. Now I'm being taken to Boston—specifically to Lydia's house. On the drive, they keep repeating the same thing: Don't worry, you're safe now. But am I? Will I be safe with Lydia, the woman who once put her fingers inside me and then burned me with her cigarettes? I whisper the question to myself, knowing no one is truly listening. They talk about taking me to a hospital and keep asking random questions, watching how I respond. It's strange how I spent almost two years with Oswaldo and no one ever called or wrote, yet now, suddenly, everyone wants to know what happened.

I stare out the window, quietly hoping for a crash, wondering if it would be better not to survive. Maybe this is the moment to run away. When they stop for gas or a bathroom break, perhaps I can disappear along the highway. Would someone pick me up? Will they accept sex in return? That's all I have to offer. I don't know what else I can give. I feel like I don't belong anywhere. Everyone moved on when I left Puerto Rico. I'm not needed to make my brother happy anymore, and Leilani is safe. There's no reason for me to stay.

I don't want to be trapped in this vehicle with my mother and brother. The windows are closed, and the air feels heavy. I crack one slightly to get a breath of fresh air, but my mother quickly tells me to close it because my new sister is sick. So, I am. I feel like throwing up. My thoughts are screaming louder than their voices, trying to drown everything out, but now it's overwhelming. I can't be here. I'm afraid of what Boston will bring. I need to flee before it's too late. Time never seems to be on my side. As we pass a green highway sign reading what seems like a warning: Massachusetts welcomes you.

There's a full house in Lydia's small apartment; people came to meet us. After this unplanned trip, I'm exhausted. I think we all are. I've become the hot topic of the family, and they're not even blood related. I feel like a rare animal in a circus, being watched from a distance while they invent my life story. The funny thing is no one knows it. I haven't told anyone, and who could know it better than me? We're all crammed into a one-bedroom apartment. Lydia has the bedroom; meanwhile, my mother and her six kids share the living room. Lydia isn't the same person I remember. She is sick and needs dialysis. She is losing her vision and already has one prosthetic eye. As if life itself is collecting her debt, her fingers are being amputated one by one. I'm grateful for God's judgment upon her. She put her fingers inside of me, and now they're being cut off. She deserves it.

My stepdad will be joining us soon, making it seven people in the living room. I don't understand why my mom bothered to bring me here. The only reason she came to United States is that her parents are old and sick. Lydia volunteered my mom to be the caretaker. Honestly, I don't think she even cares.

At this point, everyone's making assumptions about what's next. They've all invented a version of the story in which they are the rescuers. Suddenly, everyone's an expert on my story. They swear they saved me, but really, they just moved my cage to another place. All for their own good.

Now Everyone Knows

11

If you say, "But we knew nothing about this,"
does not he who weighs the heart perceive it?
Does not he who guards your life know it?
Will he not repay everyone according
to what they have done?

Proverbs 24:12 NIV

My baby sister is sick, and Mom is taking her to the hospital. She asked me to go with her. I didn't want to, but she kept insisting. We arrived at Boston City Hospital. It looks like a fancy place, but it doesn't feel like one. It's big, surrounded by tall buildings and homeless people. Once we got there, my mom registered her and went in alone with my sister. She didn't need me to come. I stayed behind in the waiting room, surrounded by sick grown-up strangers. A few minutes later, a nurse came out and called my name. I followed her into a small room with just two chairs. She left without saying much and closed the door. The room has no windows. I came to be with my mom, and we're not even in the same room. Something feels off, my heart is pounding, and I feel like I'm in danger. Why else would they leave me here?

My mom tricked me into coming to the hospital. She used my little sister as an excuse and played with my emotions. With her low, shy tone of voice, she pretended to need my help. I hate it when she changes her tone like that; if you're not paying attention, you'll fall for it. She didn't need me. This was planned: acting like she cared so I would walk into the hospital willingly. I fell for her trap.

Oswaldo was right. Her plan was to take me to a hospital as soon as we arrived in Boston, and she did just that. If she cared, why didn't she take me to the hospital in Pennsylvania? They had a city hospital too. I was naive and fell for her soft, low voice tone. She's still the same person I escaped from in Puerto Rico. So how did I end up with her again? Oswaldo warned me she will never protect me. Now I'm alone; she chose for me, and I can't go back with Oswaldo.

I think my mother is sending me to a psychiatric hospital, just like Oswaldo warned me. I can't breathe; the door is closed. I sit on the floor, in the corner between two walls, just like I used to sit beside the dog. Pretending to be in the closet, my heart slows down, and I can breathe again. Then someone knocks on the door, and I get startled. A woman enters and tells me to sit in the chair. She takes the other one and moves it close to mine. She introduces herself, holding a notebook and a pen in her hand. She says everything is "confidential" and that I can trust her. That means she's not allowed to tell anyone else.

The social worker starts talking, but I'm not really listening, mostly because I don't understand. She asks, do you want to tell me what happened at your sister's house? Why did you say you were sexually abused? Did you get sexually assaulted? Did someone touch you in a way you didn't want?

The problem is, I do not know what sexual abuse is. Nor understand the terms "molested," "sexually assaulted," or "penetration." Something bad happened to me, but I don't have the words to describe it. So, my answer was no to everything. I never said I was sexually abused; my mom did. Everyone wants me to keep their secrets, and I want to tell someone the truth, but I'm afraid to talk. I want to ask, am I really going to jail? If so, will it be a jail for kids or for adults? If they don't send me to jail, am I too old to be put up for adoption? Who can I trust and ask these things? As for now, it feels safer to stay silent.

Everyone listens to my mother's version. No one wants to hear mine. They keep coming at me with the same yes-or-no questions, just waiting for me to confirm the story they have already written.

My mother tricked me into bringing me into this hospital, and the nurse tricked me by leading me into this empty room when I'm not even a patient. Now this woman is asking questions just to write down the answers. I slid back down to the floor and breathed quietly. I stopped listening. It's just me in the dark, inside my imaginary closet.

My mother was advised to bring me for a psychiatric assessment. Just like the woman at the emergency room, this therapist has a notebook and far too many questions. I stood up and told her I wasn't answering anything about my sister or her husband. I will not talk to anyone about what happened. They're all saying I was sexually abused; I never said such a thing. It was my mother. Since she and her family always talk about my so-called "sexual abuse case."

I told the therapist I wouldn't answer anything else. I know she's not truly confidential when she's writing everything down. Then I agreed to answer as long as it wasn't about Pennsylvania. She asked me to sit and get comfortable, but how could I? The room is a mess, with papers, books, and files everywhere. This doesn't resemble a healing place. I told her I couldn't stay long; it's dirty in here. The mess reminds me of Emilia's house. The only thing missing are the roaches, for now.

Do you want to die? she asked. Yes, of course. I would rather not live with Lydia or my mother. Lydia used to put her fingers inside me. I would like to die. I'm not going to kill myself; nothing works if God wants you to stay alive. The only way out would be to run away and prostitute myself in the park. But still, I prefer to die. I want to die. I want to die.

On our way home, my mom told me she was supposed to drop me off at a hospital for crazy people to be admitted. What did you tell her, Brenda? she asked in her soft, fake-sweet voice. You're not going to kill yourself, right? I'm not going to take you to the hospital because I know you won't do it. I know you don't want to be with all those crazy people. But you have to promise you'll be good, and you won't do anything foolish. Don't be selfish; think of your sisters.

Everyone is so caught up in the Oswaldo situation that no one cares about how I feel. No one hears me when I say I don't want to stay with my mom. She dragged me out of Emilia's house and brought me here, as she had already planned this whole drama about abuse. They've been telling everyone what supposedly happened to me, but she never asked me. She never once heard my side of the story. How does everyone know? How did the hospital find out? What is sexual abuse? Why won't anyone explain what's going on?

I can't take it anymore. I need to ask her even if she slaps me. Carefully, I ask, how do you know something happened if I never told you anything? She replies, oh, remember when they came to Puerto Rico to visit? During that time, Oswaldo's mom talked to me and warned me not to let you go with them to the United States. She overheard them talking about you and told me to keep you away because they were going to do something to you. I didn't think they would actually do it; I trusted them. It's not my fault; I didn't know.

She added, I walked in on you two having sex. Don't you remember? I mean, you were just there; you stared at me. You were shocked since I caught you. You weren't being raped because you weren't fighting him off. So, I left the room and called Lydia to tell her.

There's always someone coming in and out of the house. Everyone asks, has she said anything? Have they contacted you? My sisters Aida and Mara called from Puerto Rico, along with Manny. How ironic! One popular phrase floats around all of them: I knew he was going to rape you. We saw it coming; he was always a womanizer.

Lydia told my mom she should let Tanairi and me hang out so we could make new friends and get to know the area. The only place we knew where to go was the convenience store, where we bought milk for our sisters and cigarettes and beers for the adults. We walked around the block and eventually made friends. It felt good to taste some kind of freedom. That was until my stepdad arrived from Puerto Rico and went around the block telling people not to trust me. He said I was a whore who slept with my brother-in-law and was now trying to put him in jail out of spite. Gossip travels fast. It wasn't just family anymore; now the entire neighborhood knew.

I went to my friend's house, and before I could even say hello, one of the fathers pulled me aside. He asked, you want to be my son's friend?. I said yes. He looked me up and down and said, I know who you are. We all know. Your dad came by and told us how you like to sleep with married men. I'm married. If you want to be friends with my son, you'll have to sleep with me. Otherwise, go away. I don't want my son hanging around with a whore. If you don't, I'll tell everyone who you are, and no one will let you near their kids.

I walked away heartbroken. As long as my stepdad is alive, people will hear his version of me. His life's purpose is to put women down. He's like a pebble in a shoe; small enough to make walking painful, but once removed, it becomes irrelevant.

I woke up in the middle of the night convinced Oswaldo was in the apartment. I could see his silhouette, feel him getting closer, staring at me. I've been awake ever since. I told Tanairí I thought he was here. She got scared and hid under the blanket. I stayed awake, on guard, breathing quietly, hoping he might change his mind and walk away. But exhaustion eventually pulled me under. While asleep, I took off my clothes. I couldn't breathe; as always, he felt so heavy on top of me. I screamed, though I knew no one would listen. I do in case someone feels pity for me. It never works; no one hears. Then suddenly, everyone woke up. Apparently, I had been screaming in my sleep. It was only a nightmare; still, I got undressed for him.

My mom kept asking why I took off my clothes. She didn't believe me when I said I saw Oswaldo. She was mad because I knew my brother and stepdad were sleeping in the same room, and I woke them up. I didn't mean to. It wasn't on purpose. Oswaldo was here.

All day, they've been talking about me and how I woke up screaming. As always, they talk among themselves but never to me. If I get close, they go quiet. They asked my mom to call someone and explain how hard it is to deal with me. So, she did. She called a social worker and asked for help. Not for me, but for herself, because she needs an apartment. Meanwhile, I'm left with my thoughts. No one asked me what happened last night. Was it a nightmare or something real? I don't remember undressing. I don't understand why it felt so real if it wasn't. I go to the bathroom and sit on the floor, like I'm being punished, sitting next to the dog. It's the only way I know how to silence everything, especially my mind. It's like I'm drowning.

Summer is almost here, and that means more hot days ahead. One of the neighbors invited us to visit Franklin Park Zoo. There was one day when the neighborhood residents could go in for free. We live just a few streets away, but it's my first time going. The animals are all in cages, pacing or lying still. The gorillas sit near the big window, soaking in the attention from the crowd. But it's the lion that captures me. He's lying on the ground with his back turned away from spectators. People think he's asleep, but I know he is not. He's awake, breathing quietly, while flicking his tail softly in an attempt to keep the bugs away. He is trying to become invisible to the crowd.

I relate to him. He's tired of being trapped, of having his vulnerability on display. People gather to talk and take pictures, but no one cares about him. He knows he can't escape. He eats what he's given. No matter how loud he roars, no one comes to rescue him. He might be the king of the jungle, but even he grows weak under the power of cruel hands. He's just like me, being punished, restrained in a cage with no explanation. No reason why. We both lost a battle we were never given the chance to fight.

Later, someone called from Pennsylvania. Following her conversation with my mother, she requested to speak with me. Her name is Judith. She assured me she'll help and I shouldn't worry. Help me with what? I'm not the one asking for help; my mother is. I just agree with whatever people say. I'm used to it. They keep asking the same questions in different ways until I respond. Maybe they should just write me a script of everything they want to hear. That way they can stop asking, and I can stop guessing the right answers.

My birthday is coming up, and I thank God that my mother never remembers it. I'll never celebrate my birthday. She is more worried about our upcoming trip to Pennsylvania. My stepfather is furious; he doesn't want her to go with me. He keeps repeating the same things: Look, Brenda, look at all the consequences of the big mess you created. Couldn't keep your legs closed? Do you think it's fair for us, for your mom to travel because of you? You think you're that important? Next time you're feeling horny, scratch your own itchy spot so no one has to clean up after you. His words have become my breakfast, lunch, and dinner. He's lucky that no one ever dares to stop him from saying what he thinks. My mother just nods and smiles. I knew it the moment I saw her, didn't I tell you? That daughter of yours is a whore. I was right. She couldn't even respect her sister. You hit the jackpot with Brenda. What a prize!

Judith called again and asked if I had any questions. I said yes. Why do I have to go back to Pennsylvania? Can you ask them to take me back? I don't want to live with my mom. Judith said she would explain more when we meet in person. Your mother already told you, didn't she? No, she didn't, I said. I don't know what's happening. No one wants to tell me anything. She mentioned I could fly by myself if my mother couldn't come since she has a sick baby. I told her that I'm big and almost twelve and that I want to travel alone. But no one seems to listen. What do I know? They're the experts, right?

Talking to my mom about going alone isn't worth it. She says she has to go, or they'll think she doesn't care. She's not risking social services opening a case because of me. She didn't expect the law to require us to press charges in Pennsylvania. Nothing will be done in Boston, and now it's too late for her to back out.

For the first time in my life, my mother gave me money to buy clothes for school. It wasn't much, but I was able to get a pair of jeans and two shirts. Still, I know nothing is ever truly free. One way or another, I'll have to repay her.

It's a strange feeling, this quiet excitement about starting school. I wonder if I'll do well or if I'll end up sick like my brother. Now that we're living in the same place again, that fear has returned. Emilia once wanted to take me to a therapist, not because she cared, but because she could get extra money if I was diagnosed with a mental condition. She said if they gave me pills, I'd officially be considered crazy. Oswaldo didn't want me to see a therapist or take medication. He said he didn't support her plan because he knew I wasn't crazy. As awful as that sounds, it meant something to me. He might have been the only person who believed I was sane. That small, twisted comfort made me overlook all the harm he caused.

I don't know who I am or who I want to be. It's like everyone is waiting for me to fall apart, just so they can say I'm broken. Maybe it would be easier for them if I was. Even though they crafted a public version of my story, I hold on to my truth. I have it hidden like a buried treasure, waiting for that day I can finally expose it myself. For everyone to know all the things they did in secret.

A Date to Remember

12

But if the man meets the engaged woman out in the country,
and he rapes her, then only the man must die.
Do nothing to the young woman; she has committed
no crime worthy of death. She is as innocent as
a murder victim. Since the man raped her out in the country,
it must be assumed that she screamed,
but there was no one to rescue her.

Deuteronomy 22:25-27 NLT

All my stepfather talks about is how we are required to travel to Pennsylvania. August 27th feels like a cursed day, though I still don't understand why it's my fault. I wish my mother could see me as a human being and actually talk to me. I ask questions and get no answers. My stepfather does all the talking for her, and it's never anything good. He points fingers at me like he's trying to hide his flaws. My mother is a coward who hides behind silence.

Today is the day, and we're on our way to the bus terminal. My mother, my baby sister, and I will be traveling from Massachusetts to the state of Pennsylvania. We get on a big bus named after a famous cartoon movie, and I feel lost just like the character. The seats are big and somewhat comfortable, but that's all there is. We stop in New York before heading to our final destination.

The ride is long; I'm bored and tired. At the beginning, my mother gave me the silent treatment because she was mad, she had to come with me and leave her lover behind. This trip is so inconvenient for them; I am still a hindrance for her. My sister is tired of sitting, and there's nothing to do. My mother must be getting bored, too, because now she's trying to talk to me. I decided to give her the same silent treatment. We have nothing to say to each other.

I see the road signs announcing Reading, Pennsylvania, and it terrifies me. How can she bring me back here? Still, as crazy as it sounds, I'd rather be with Oswaldo. He doesn't owe me anything since we're not blood related. My mother, on the other hand, should have protected me. Calm my brother down and stood up to her lover. If she saw me having sex with Oswaldo, why call Lydia and not the police? Why did she stay silent with the businessman?

We arrived at the bus terminal in Reading, Pennsylvania, where Judith greeted us. She was a white American woman with soft blonde hair who spoke gently and politely. She drove us to her office in a minivan. At one point, she asked if I wanted to listen to any specific music. I didn't have a preference; I just silently hoped she wouldn't play that song, the one that reminds the bad men of me. Still, it was nice of her to ask. She even turned on the air conditioner. I stared out the window, taking in the strange feeling of riding in a car and being free to look outside.

Then suddenly, she asked me to put my head down or look out the other way. Look away, Brenda, look away! And there he was, standing right in front of the house. From his face, I could tell Oswaldo hadn't expected to see us, to see me. He looked confused, and I was just as stunned. He stared straight into my eyes. Did time stop? Judith kept driving, but we were locked in a strange, silent staring contest. Did they bring me back to him because of my birthday? Oh no. Why are they doing this to me? No, please, no!

I could hear Judith's voice in the background, distant like a fading echo. Brenda, take a deep breath. Can you talk to me? But I couldn't answer. I felt frozen, completely paralyzed. I was far away from him, yet I could feel his presence like he was right beside me. I couldn't move as if I was trapped in time, in a memory, trapped in fear.

Slowly, I start to come back. Sitting on the floor in what looks like a play area. There are toys and coloring pages scattered around. I wonder if the dog peed in his corner. I'm sure no one has cleaned his area. He must be feeling lonely, wondering what he did wrong.

After Judith finished talking to my mom, she came over to me. I was still stuck at the crossroads, caught somewhere between my brother-in-law, the closet, and this office. She handed me a small cup of cold water, and as I drank, she gently asked me to come sit at the big meeting table. My mother traded places with me. Judith had so many questions. I was in an automatic mode when I answered, pointing to certain body parts. Speaking words, I couldn't fully grasp. Not being mentally present. I needed more time to feel safe enough to return. I didn't mean to speak, but I did.

Judith switched from writing in a notebook to a large portfolio filled with papers. A man joined us. He'll be working with us, they said. He came and went. I didn't remember him from earlier, and I didn't catch his name. He asked questions, flipping through the papers, exchanging them back and forth. They said they must move fast since we don't have much time before we head back to Boston.

Eventually, they took us to a shelter to spend the night. It was a place for victims of domestic violence. I remember when Emilia had a fight with her husband and he hit her. She let me tag along, and we ended up sleeping at a shelter. The next morning, she called him from a public phone, and we all went back to the apartment. There should be a place like that for kids to stay for a few nights, feel warmth, eat hot meals, and maybe talk to a free counselor. A place to clear your mind and regain a little strength. I only get offered an evaluation and a bed in a mental hospital. When I say I would rather not live with my mom, they just tell me I need more time to adjust.

Early in the morning, we were picked up and taken to a clinic. The doctor works for the court and was on my side. That's what they say.

The nurse called me into a room and left me alone for me to change into a hospital gown. Not understanding why, I keep being taken to hospitals. I haven't said I am sick; no one knows I can't breathe or about my heart problems. When I feel unwell, I sit on the floor pretending I am inside the closet until I catch my breath, or my heart slows down.

The doctor comes in and tells me it will be quick, that she'll try not to make me uncomfortable. She asks me to lie back and slide toward the edge of this strange little bed, then she grabs my feet and place them in some weird holders, telling me to relax since my legs are shaking. What is she doing? Is she going to hurt me? I feel pain as she touches me and inserts something, and I instinctively slide up to the top. She tries again, promising to be gentle. But why is she touching me? Why do I have to be naked? It's like my body doesn't belong to me. People just take it when they want. The doctor keeps saying to relax, so I run far away in my mind. When I open my eyes, I feel disoriented. Is she done using me? Who dressed me? I hear her talking to Judith, saying she prescribed some antibiotics and that she felt sorry for me. I hate it when people feel sorry. They don't know me. They only feel sorry for my mom's version of the story, not mine.

We returned to Judith's office, and David was there waiting. I'm slowly walking back into reality, not rushing. I know I'll have to run again. David handed Judith a newspaper, and they read it together. Oswaldo's name was in it; he had tried to run from the police, but he still was arrested. I wondered if he was preparing the drugs and maybe didn't have time to flush them down the toilet. Did he beat up another addict or sell to the wrong cop? I'm glad I wasn't the one on lookout. I would've been in serious trouble.

This time, my mom stayed in the playroom with my little sister while I sat with Judith and David. They had a long list of questions; I didn't understand most of them. One of them was, what happened in October? I don't know. October cold winds were pulling leaves off the trees. Judith said that my mom told them about October. Then David asked, Brenda, can you tell us what happened the first time Oswaldo had sex with you? No! No, no, I'll get sick. Why does everyone want to know? I hate my mom. Why is she talking about me? Don't listen to her. She wants the police to take me to jail. Stop asking questions. Stop! Why is everyone talking about me? Why does everyone blame me? I can't breathe.

Do I know what happened in October? Is she talking about that day she invited me to the park and started asking questions in her soft, friendly voice? Earlier that day, Oswaldo had taken me to his room and was having sex with me when my mom walked in. I remember seeing her face from a distance; it's all a blur. Was she really standing there? I remember her turning away, giving me her back. Oswaldo leaned over and whispered, now she'll take you to the hospital and send you to jail or a mental institution. Later that day, she took me to the park and started asking questions.

I found myself alone in the room as I opened my eyes. Judith came in and offered me a cup of water. Sitting on the floor beside me, she asked me to play Connect Four with her. I didn't answer, so she started playing on her own. After a few rounds, I joined her. I know how it feels when no one wants to play with you. While we played, Judith told me they were there to help and why she trusted David. They had worked together for a long time, helping kids like me. She asked if it would be okay for him to come in and join us. When she opened the door, he was already standing outside, waiting anxiously.

While playing, David asked if I was afraid of going to jail. I told him yes. He asked why, and I said, because I was his girlfriend. Oswaldo told me that if I ever tell anyone, the police will lock me up for fifteen years. David looked at me and said, you can trust me; I won't let that happen. Oswaldo got arrested for what he did. Brenda, the police know, and they didn't arrest you. You're safe.

David, did the police rescue the dog? Can you help the dog if I talk? I think the dog wants to be rescued. He's scared of Oswaldo and always cries. But no one can get to him; he's tied up in the basement near the Indian. You can't go down there, because the Indian will take your blood. If Oswaldo kills you with the knife, he'll give your blood to the Indian, and no one will ever find you. I get scared when I'm punished and tied up in front of the Indian. He seems to be alive; is scary. I don't want to talk about the Indian anymore.

Oswaldo said that if he got in trouble with the police, he would tell them about the box. So, I guess it is ok to talk now.

He asked if I was willing to answer some of those questions in front of more people. He promised that he would not let anyone hurt me. Oswaldo will be there too, but I don't have to look at him. I told David I was ready. He said that because of me, Oswaldo would never be able to hurt anyone else.

Judith brought me back to the playroom. I didn't speak to my mother, not wanting her to know about me. If she finds out, she'll tell her sister Lydia, and my stepdad will make sure the whole neighborhood hears about it. We spent most of the day in that room. Judith asked what we wanted to eat; she was ordering food for us. I didn't dare ask for anything, so she ordered Chinese food and pizza.

I hate Chinese food; it makes me sick. That is Oswaldo's celebration food. For a moment, she almost ruined my day. But I chose to stay focused. I will talk in front of more people, so no other child gets punished like me. Even if the police arrest me, I will save others, and that should be reason enough to celebrate.

David returned with a light in his eyes. Brenda, you'll be happy when I tell you the news. The police went back to the house and found the dog in the basement; they rescued him. The police also found the knives and the Indian, and they took care of it. You don't need to be afraid. I promise Oswaldo is the only one going to jail. You are safe.

If only someone had spoken, I would not be in this situation, if only someone had listened. One voice is what it takes to rescue someone, only one listener. For one person not to turn a blind eye.

The court hearing is set for late in the evening. As the time was getting closer, Judith took us to another location. They keep asking if I'm ready. I'm not. I still think it's unfair the way I was taken to the hospital in Boston, just because my mother decided to follow the advice of her so-called family. She tricked me, dropping a heavy burden onto my shoulders. She chose a path that requires courage, then washed her hands and left me behind to finish the job.

Earlier, I felt proud of myself, brave for a moment. Now I feel afraid. What if Oswaldo already told the police about the dirty secrets? Is he going to mention the box, the one he put me in with his son? About the day I was on top of him? Will they laugh when he tells them how I ate off the floor?

I waited in a small room with Judith. As they called me, I walked inside the courtroom alone. I'm scared; my body is trembling. I wasn't expecting this many people. The small courtroom is packed. People are standing outside, peering through the door; there isn't any more room on the benches. Emilia and Will are sitting among the audience, staring at me. I can feel her anger and the worry in him. My mother is sitting with a group of people I don't recognize. She is a stranger just like them. Oswaldo is right up front at a small table, calm like nothing's wrong. Everyone is watching me, some with anger, some with pity.

David said to look at him whenever I needed support, promising to be right by my side. I can't find him. Before I answer the first question, I catch a glimpse of my mother walking out. I'm alone, abandoned in a full room. Wait, I found him! David is sitting at a table in the front row. I'm not alone after all!

I am seated in the front row, adjacent to the judge. They ask me to state my name as I raise my hand and swear to tell the truth. My hand is shaking, and so is my voice. I need to take a deep breath, just like Judith taught me. This was my mother's idea, and she turned her back on me. How can it hurt and also feel like a relief at the same time? I'm glad she's gone. I don't want her to hear what I have to say.

David asks me a few questions. He wants to know if Oswaldo is present in the courtroom. While David speaks to me, it feels like we're alone, and I can reply like I did back in the office. Then another man stands up to ask questions. Suddenly, David gets lost in the crowd; I can't find him.

The man asks, Did Oswaldo rape you? No, he didn't, I say. Instantly everyone starts talking. I can't breathe. The judge bangs his gavel, but the noise keeps rising.

—Brenda, did Oswaldo rape you?
No, he did not, I repeat, still gasping for air.

I spot David talking to the judge. Minutes felt like forever before everyone returned to their seats. The courtroom goes silent again. The man looks at me and asks, If Oswaldo didn't rape you, does that mean you agreed to be his girlfriend?

—I didn't want to be his girlfriend. No! He got mad when I said no. He had sex with me, and then I agreed because he hit me and held a knife near my face. He told me he would cut me and give the Indian my blood if I didn't stop shaking. I obeyed by holding my legs.

As I try to explain, the man keeps interrupting. It's a yes or no question. Just answer yes or no. It's difficult to talk to this man. He asks questions, then gets mad when I try to answer.

—This is a yes or no question! That's not what I'm asking! How many times did he have sex with you? If you're telling the truth, how can you not know how many times? His questions piled up, and I don't have answers. This is a mistake; I don't even know what happened. What is my mother's version? I said that Oswaldo is present, and now I am being questioned. I must stand up and point at Oswaldo to make sure that we're talking about the same person. I don't want to. Judith told me I did not have to look at him. There is no one on my side. I try to find David or Judith, but I keep losing them. I feel ashamed talking about how he had sex with me while everyone is listening. Now they all know I am not a virgin.

This feels more like a circus; I am the main attraction. All eyes are on me. I lift my face for a few seconds, but the weight of guilt pulls it right back down. There isn't a single person here for me. My mother left. Why did she come? I glance at the door, hoping she might be peaking like the others, but she's not. Instead, I see Orlando, Oswaldo's younger brother. We lock eyes, he smiles at me, and I smile back.

The man interrupts my silence. —Can you find Oswaldo?

I still have my eyes on Orlando. He takes a breath and nods. I know he wants me to do it, to point out his brother like they're asking. So, I stood up. Raising my shaking hand, I point straight at him. Oswaldo bursts into laughter, and while a smile is drawn on his face, a tear slides down my cheek. I glance back at Orlando, and he is still smiling, giving me a thumb-up.

Even though Orlando isn't here to support me, he might be the only one in the crowd who does. I stare at him, and every time they ask a question, I don't answer unless he nods his head. That's his silent way of saying it's okay to talk, similar to when no one was around. He'd signal that it was safe to use the bathroom, to take a sip of water, or to take a bite of food. This won't last forever, he used to say. He stands by my side from a distance, breathing in as I speak, smiling when I finish. He reminds me I'm not alone. This won't last forever!

The questions don't seem to end, but finally, they do. I feel the tiniest wave of relief when I'm allowed to stand and walk to the backroom. When the guard opens the courtroom door and then closes it behind me, I collapse in the hallway.

I sit on the floor to catch my breath. Judith tells me it's better to wait in the room, helping me to get on my feet. We waited as the evening turned into night. When David comes back, they all congratulate each other. For them, this is a victory. It went better than expected. Especially since there's no way my brother-in-law would be able to pay the two-hundred-thousand-dollar bail. My mother reappeared for the celebration.

We were about to leave the court through a back door, as if we were escaping or going hiding. When the judge called my name while catching up to us. He would like to have a few words with me.

I'm thinking this will be the moment of my arrest. It is now time for me to be punished. I will not try to run like Oswaldo did. After all, I did ask my nephew to touch me and kiss me while we were inside the box. It is my fault!

A few times Oswaldo gave me a chance; he would say, it is up to you if we have sex or not. I will give you one minute, two minutes, or three minutes to push me off. I will not penetrate you during that time frame. If you push me off, I will get dressed. But... If you don't push me off, I will penetrate you as soon as the time is up. Each time, I would do everything I could to push him off me. Every single time my strength was accompanied by a scream. I would feel all my energy evaporating through my pores while I gave my one hundred percent. Every single time, I failed. Oswaldo didn't even put in an effort to match his strength with mine. I was so weak, I never succeeded in pushing him off. Failure always arrived in a chariot, and guilt followed behind, dragging its chains like an uninvited guest. It's your fault, Oswaldo used to say. You provoke me to do these things.

I take a deep breath, looking at the judge, bracing for his verdict.

The judge tells me, I'm very proud of you. You did well; you are a strong and brave young girl. I preferred not to say this in front of everyone. I want you to know that this will be a date I will always remember. You must be special. He locked you in a closet, but you stood up. Using the power of your voice, you have shackled him for the rest of his life. You must have a purpose when life gives you this kind of victory as a gift on this date.
The judge smiles as he walks away and tells me, Happy Birthday!

 The date I was born, as a hindrance in my mother's life, marked the day someone went to prison. They all called it justice, but I didn't see it that way because I couldn't comprehend the crime that was done to me. I only saw how I was used as a pawn on the game board of others, left with the sting of punishment and a new wound in a life already full of scars. Maybe at that moment I was only longing for love and not justice.

The Judgment of Men

13

What sorrow for those who say that evil is good
and good is evil, that dark is light and light is dark,
that bitter is sweet and sweet is bitter.
What sorrow for those who are wise
in their own eyes and think themselves so clever.
What sorrow for those who are heroes at drinking wine
and boast about all the alcohol they can hold.
They take bribes to let the wicked go free,
and they punish the innocent.

Isaiah 5:20-23 NLT

My mother, my sister, and I travel back to the state of Pennsylvania one more time. This time, to an elegant courthouse in a tall building. The inside is clean, with shiny floors that reflect the lights above. The lobby alone looks like a museum. Here, I must testify in front of the jury, his family, friends, and strangers. The courtroom has plenty of seats; no one is left standing or peeking through the door. Even so, my mom decides to leave when it is my time to speak.

Not all the questions are yes or no; now they want details. I do my best to answer, to give them what they're asking for, while struggling to stay focused. Oswaldo is sitting right in front of me at a small table. Every time I speak, he laughs, and I can hear him. They've placed me in the witness stand, surrounded by a small wooden cubicle, so I managed to hide my shaking body. I think he can only see my shoulders and face. I can hide my body, but not my voice. Everyone hears the great fear in my trembling voice.

Occasionally, the judge allows a short break. As soon as I step out into the hallway leading to our waiting room, my legs give out, and I sit on the floor to breathe in silence. At one point, Oswaldo laughs so loudly that I burst into tears. The judge permits David to escort me back to the break room. I can't stop crying. He laughs to show me that he still has power over me, a reminder that I am weak and he is strong. His laughter tells me that no matter how much I scream or fight, no one will come. To him, this is a game. Even when losing is inevitable, he still plays to win. And somehow, he makes me feel like I'm the one who's failing. After all, I'm all alone. It's him against me.

The day he was sentenced, we weren't present at court. I didn't even know it was an option for me to witness his reaction. Did he laugh when he heard the word guilty? No one ever tells me what the steps are. I was just being dragged through the whole process.

That day, the phone rang; it's Judith calling. After my mother hangs up, she walks over to my stepdad and Lydia first, then finally comes to me. Brenda, he was found guilty. We did it! My mom is very excited. All the adults agreed that it's a time to celebrate with alcoholic drinks.

The seven charges are as follows:

- Rape, Forcible Compulsion — Guilty
- Statutory Rape — Guilty
- Victim Less Than 16 Years Old — Guilty
- Indecent Assault (Over 18 / Under 14) — Guilty
- Indecent Exposure — Guilty
- Endangering Welfare of a Child — Guilty
- Corruption of Minors — Guilty

Oswaldo was sentenced to eighteen years in prison.

While my mother celebrates, I get trapped in a storm of emotions, feeling lost. Torturing my mind with the same question. What about Emilia? The trial was over, he was condemned to incarceration, and I was condemned to silence. There's a difference between answering questions based on my mother's version and telling my story. Who will listen to my story?

My stepfather took it upon himself to build my reputation. It's like everyone already knows his version of me: Brenda, the whore who sleeps with any man, even her sister's husband. I'm constantly being sexually harassed. It's exhausting when people ask me if it's true. His friends flash their genitals at me, thinking I'll spread my legs. They toss coins on the floor and ask what sexual favor I'm willing to do. Because of him, they all see me as nothing more than a sex doll.

I am getting bullied at school because my stepfather went with my mom and told the teacher in front of the class that I was working as a stripper. The teacher should call social services to make a report, since I am twelve years old. But instead, the Spanish teacher decides to listen to the gossip and then uses me as an example in front of the whole class. When I got home, I questioned my mother about why she stood there while he told lies about me. I also reminded her that her "soulmate" is not my father.

There's no point in talking to my mother. She'd make the perfect mute, silent when confronted and silent in the face of injustice. I hardly spend time with my sisters anymore because my stepfather constantly threatens me. He calls me a whore with a mental problem and says he doesn't want them getting "infected" by me. If I even get close to them, he pulls me aside and says, I'm watching you. If they turn into whores like you, I'll break your face. Get away from them; I don't want them to be like you. Why do you want to be near them? So, they can be whores like you? You're worthless, you know that, right? If they follow in your footsteps, I'll hit you like a man. I'll break your face. He is a weak, miserable old man. It is with my mom's silence that his words gain power over me.

I must admit that my mother might have changed. I see her trying to be better with my sisters. In Boston, I am not the slave I have been in Puerto Rico. My brother is in a mental institution, so I am no longer responsible for his care or medications. My mother always has food for my sisters and doesn't disappear for days at a time. I no longer had to go searching for her or deal with businessmen. Still, there were days I preferred to starve rather than eat at home, just to avoid the constant reminder: the food is for the girls. In Pennsylvania, I learned to eat everything I could at school. What other kids considered disgusting school lunch, to me it was manna from heaven.

Weekends were filled with gatherings, my mom, Lydia, and friends drinking and blasting music from the evening until the next morning. Lydia demanded I show her respect and even wanted me to ask for her blessing like she was some holy saint. I followed my mother's lead and gave her the silent treatment. No matter what they said, I refused to reply. Additionally, I was learning how to express myself sarcastically. After she lost her vision and fingers due to her medical condition, I took pleasure in making remarks about it. Those nights were long and sleepless, with migraines that kept me up. But I turned to God and thanked Him, because now she had no fingers left to molest and no vision left to lust.

My mother always stayed silent. The woman who once held so much power over me had become weak and powerless in my eyes by the time I was twelve years old. It's as if all her choices are shaped by the opinions of her lover and Lydia. Sometimes, I even feel sorry for her.

The therapists agreed that I needed time to adjust; after all, I hadn't lived with my mom for two years. They said I needed to get to know my little sisters and bond with them. We had moved to a new state, and supposedly the most important thing now was for me to accept that my mom is entitled to be happy with a man. I grew up without a father figure, and I can't afford to rebel now just because she's in a relationship. Living with her again means I have to deal with all these feelings. Does the therapist really think that is my problem?

While the therapist brainstorms ideas to help me "accept" things, I stay silent. Where does she get her information from? Does she know I'm being sexually harassed by men because of the gossip my stepfather spreads? Does she know that the only way my mom and I connect is when we drink alcohol? That I do not have any underwear, and neighbors laugh in my face, saying my stepfather told them my panties are stained? One old woman even gave me a lecture on how girls used to know how to hand-wash their clothes back in the day. Why is he talking about my underwear at all? Is this normal?

People judge me based on the version they were told. I am losing my identity; I don't even know who I am anymore. I've been labeled so many things: a burden, the ugly one, the rebellious one. Then there are the medical and social labels: victim, depression, anxiety, and PTSD. Everyone seems to know who I am, except me. Words have become bricks, building a wall around me. Silence is the glue that seals those bricks together. A wall reinforced with shame, guilt, and judgment that seems impossible to escape. A fortress of shame that I never asked to live in. Yet here I am.

I told my mother I wanted to become a therapist. She laughed, saying therapists are crazy, and told me I should become a hairstylist instead. Just like that, I lost all interest in school. I had hoped I could help other kids, listen to them without judgment, and give them what no one ever gave me. But now, the fear of becoming mentally unstable like my brother weighs heavier than any dream I once had. Emilia has to be mentally ill; Aida and Mara must be too. Realizing that made the fear grow even louder in my mind. What if mental illness runs in the family?

Instead of going to school, I wander around Boston. I walk the streets, talking to strangers. In a twisted way, I'm hoping to be kidnapped by a sex trafficker. I know I'm too old to be rescued by a loving family like in the movies. But at twelve, I'm still young enough to be wanted by perverts. That's the only thing I seem to be good for. I must have some invisible superpower that attracts predators, and I don't know how to turn it off. Like an animal that gives off a scent only perverts can detect. Depraved people catch it in the air like someone hunting for its prey. They stay on the lookout for the small, the weak, and the wounded. They go after the easy prey, and I am precisely all of that. An abandoned, lonely, and wounded animal.

I belong to a family of nine siblings, yet I am alone. There's no one I can talk to or trust. I'm drowning, flailing in deep water with no lifeguard in sight. Everyone is busy trying to stay afloat, caught up in their pain, trying to survive. No one sees me, and the few who do… are drowning too.

I have a friend at school, and we often walk home together. We laugh and share stories, but when we get near her house, we hide. Her mom doesn't allow her to have friends. She's from Honduras, and I think we have more in common than we realize. Her mother doesn't love her. She's cold unless a certain family friend is around. A man in his mid-forties with a family of his own. He brings them money and gifts, especially when he sleeps with my friend. My friend thinks he loves her. I know he is a businessman. Who am I to say? When you never receive love, even a crumb feels like an entire meal.

I also grew close to a boy from school who lives close by. His mom is a single mother of three and expects him to take care of everything. Like her personal babysitter, he does the housework and takes care of the sisters while she works. Still, nothing he does is enough, as she hits him often. I watch him sink deeper into depression each day, like someone slowly disappearing beneath the surface. One day, he told me he wanted to end his life. He listed every reason he had, his mom being the number one. Then he asked me, do you think there's help for kids like us? Put yourself in my shoes. Would you try to get help, or would you rather kill yourself? I told him there's no help for kids like us. At least I haven't found it yet.

Less than an hour later, people gathered outside. Someone found him dead, hanging from a tree.

If you are contemplating ending your life, seek help. Today's pain does not have to define your future. Call or text **Suicide & Crisis Lifeline # 988**

My sister Emilia moved to Boston from Pennsylvania. One of the first things she asked was if I was HIV positive. When I told her no, she said that was the proof that Oswaldo didn't rape me, because she was HIV positive. Later, she blamed me for her sickness, claiming that if I had just stayed and "pleased her husband," none of this would've happened. She said if I still had any love for her, I'd go to the court and say everything was a lie. That he never raped me. A few days later, she handed me a letter from Oswaldo. He had written it from prison, and the papers were covered in blood. In the letter, his rage was aimed at my mother. The blood, he said, was symbolic. If his mother died from heartbreak over his imprisonment, then mine would pay in the same way, with blood. About me, he only wrote one thing: Brenda showed me she wanted to be with me when she smiled. It felt like a blade twisting in my chest. A smile? A smile I didn't even remember. A moment he used to justify destroying me.

I spent months going from clinic to clinic, anonymously getting tested for HIV, haunted by fear. I stopped eating, sometimes eating too much, hoping to quiet the storm inside. I cried every day, especially while waiting at the clinic. Once, a Christian pastor who worked in the clinic told me that if I didn't want to get HIV, I should stop sleeping around. I never went back to that clinic in Salem again. It took many negative results for me to believe I was healthy.

Emilia came back into my life to torture me, and she succeeded for a while. Until I realized she was never stronger than me.

For years, I lived in denial, not wanting to accept what had happened to me. Someone sneaked into my bedroom while I was asleep. That a child's game could turn into a sexual game. One person played pornographic movies to fulfill a fantasy. An old man took advantage of my desperation in the search for my mother. That a woman caused me harm and was wicked enough to burn me. Another one took advantage of the fact that my mother was drunk and publicly touched me. That one person would ask me to join my sister for sexual acts. In denial that my father would dare to compare me with my mother. That businessmen were not ethical. That my oldest sister took me as a slave to please her husband. And my childhood was stolen by all of them.

Accepting the truth opened a door that leads to the road of recovery. Peeking through that exit, the path ahead looks rough. The scenery isn't peaceful. No magical shortcut, no rainbow bridge to take me safely across. Only thunderstorms and air that spins with the threat of a tornado. A roller coaster of pain, full of endless loops. I see the faded starting line, where so many have stepped onto this path.

This road leads through dark tunnels of fear and grief. It's a race everyone wants to finish, but not everyone makes it. I see people with torn clothes from how long they have walked. Some gasping for air, others drowning in their tears. I cannot see the finish line from where I stand. But I am choosing this new road. Leaving behind my family's journey, full of secrets and judgment, I step forward in hopes of finding a better future for those who will come after me.

A Silent God

14

My complaint today is still a bitter one, and I try hard
not to groan aloud. If only I knew where to find God,
I would go to his court. I would lay out my case and present
my arguments. Then I would listen to his reply
and understand what he says to me.
Would he use his great power to argue with me? No,
He would give me a fair hearing. Honest people can reason
with him, so I would be forever acquitted by my judge.

Job 23:2-7 NLT

Every time I take a few steps on the road to recovery, I end up stopping. I've seen a few therapists, and everything is fine, that is, until I start talking. I keep getting the same reaction: it is too much trauma; you need someone with more experience. The funny thing is, I've never even told anyone the whole story. I tell minimal details to see if someone might stay, listen, and not give up on me. But most of them give up, and so do I.

There are days when tears become my breakfast, lunch, and dinner. I feel angry; many failed me. The ones who should've protected me turned their backs. There are moments I feel like society owes me something, like it was their silence that allowed me to be ignored. And yet, I get angry at myself too, every time I become like the rest of them, staying silent and burying my story. The hopelessness wraps around me, and I become helpless in front of my emotions. Fear keeps winning. I get dressed each day in a uniform of shame, walking in pain-inflicting shoes. My voice is strangled by the guilt tied around my neck like a rope. I feel paralyzed and heartbroken. They saw me exposed, naked, and wounded. Still, they walked away. I was left, agonizing and alone.

Since I was a little girl, I've been searching for something I could hold on to, something that no one could take away from me. I've been searching for someone who would accept me just as I am. Someone who would walk beside me, hear my story, and say, *you're going to be okay.* Someone I could trust, who is willing to love me, even when I feel unlovable. I need mercy. I require someone to look at me, broken as I am, and still choose to stay. But nobody goes looking for broken things to love. And I know it will take a lot to fix me. I'm not even worth saving. Who would invest in someone this shattered?

Today I decided to end my life; I see no purpose in me. The road to recovery feels impossible. I'm stuck going in circles. No matter how many steps I take, I can't move forward while I'm still carrying the secrets of others. It weighs me down; this is not a life worth living. I'm not a survivor who is surrounded by family and friends, celebrating a victory for escaping or being rescued. Currently, I'm a victim, still bound by the chains of abuse.

As a last resort, I cried out to God one more time, but even my prayer felt ignored. I searched for all the Spanish churches in Salem, Massachusetts, hoping someone might pray for me. Maybe if the request came from one of His people, God would listen. The first call went to voicemail. The second church told me their prayer night was on Tuesdays, and I was welcome to attend. The pastor's wife answered the third call. I told her I needed prayer and she was my last option. That if God didn't intervene, I would take my life. She asked if I was a member. I said no. Then she said, for me to help you, you must become a member.

I was already sitting by the window. Looking up at the sky, I whispered, God, are these your followers? You have no people here in Salem.

I went on with the plan to end this torment. There was no turning back. No hope, no God. Everyone won; they all got away with it. Each of them picked up a stone and threw it at a defenseless girl. Every stone becomes a word, a rejection, a touch, a kiss, or a punishment. They did not kill me all at once; they kept doing it slowly. One by one, stone by stone.

As I was about to carry out my plan, I collapsed to the floor. There, I broke down in tears. I didn't choose this life, and I'm the one paying for the consequences of others. I'm about to end it all, while the ones who did the damage are out there enjoying life. They'll be the same ones to act surprised and ask, why?

A commotion outside pulls my attention. I look up to seeing birds flying in wide, frantic circles. Seagulls and pigeons are common in this area, but these black birds look different, agitated, and restless. Are they fighting for food? Then I saw a single white bird flying right through the center of chaos. Suddenly I understood. God, are those black birds demons coming to take my soul to hell? Are you the white bird, finally showing me a sign? If so, it's too late now. I'm not turning back. I'm eighteen; I got to choose my destiny. I'm not afraid of hell; I've been living in it. I tried to get up, but I couldn't; my body was paralyzed. I was burning from the inside, like I was under the desert sun, boiling with rage. Yet, I was drowning in tears, like I had been thrown into the middle of the ocean. I was furious and heartbroken. The knife and the pills I had ready fell from my hands when I collapsed. I tried to reach for them, but my body wouldn't obey. There's weight preventing me from moving.

Deep down, I knew it was God. I just didn't know if He came to punish or save me. Was this my final moment before meeting Him, or would He show me mercy? I had planned to plead my case, but now I had no words. Only pain and shame. The agony of being exposed, naked before the God I thought had forgotten me. Is this what dying feels like? I could feel my heart breaking into tiny pieces. All I could whisper was, God… please… let me die.

Time stands still. I'm lying on the floor, crying my heart out. I've waited so many years to have an encounter with God, and now what? The eighteen-year-old Brenda is angry, hopeless, and done with life. But the little girl in me, the innocent one who once waited for Him under the sun, wants to scream for help. I can't stop crying. But this crying feels different. I feel allowed to cry.

God, I know you're here. I've waited so long to meet you. Where were you? I wanted to apologize for misbehaving in Heaven. I believed that lie, that maybe I deserved all this, that I had done something wrong even before I was born. I wanted to repent because I thought if I apologized, perhaps I could come back to you. Everyone blamed me for what they did to me. So, I blamed myself too. At least it gave me some kind of reason why. I still don't understand why I was born. Did you forget to give me a purpose? Why so much torture? Once would have been enough. One person would have been more than enough for me to understand pain. For two years I ran into the sky, chasing a castle, hoping to find You. I ran after you, but you kept running away; you abandoned me.

Where were you? Did you witness the injustices? Did you see me cry? Did you hear me scream? When the extension cord or the box wasn't enough, did you really send a dog to punish me? Was I bothering you when I asked for help? Were you the one protecting me that day? Why do you not let me die? Now, I am broken.

God, if you still have mercy for someone like me, I will surrender my life to you. If you take away this pain and give me a purpose, I will tell my story to honor you. If you cover my nakedness, I will speak of you. Please! Free me, heal me, and restore me. Save me.

I began to read the Bible, wanting to get to know God. Every day, I would pray, asking for someone, anyone, to invite me to a church. I was open to anything. I am willing to accept any religion. I lived in a city with several churches, yet not one person invited me. My prayers turned into complaints: there is no one in Salem who genuinely thinks the gospel is worth sharing. As I waited, I saw him as a friend. Of course I question myself: an imaginary friend at eighteen? After all, He was a silent God.

Six months later, I was finally a guest in a church. I do not remember what the sermon was about. But when the pastor made the altar call, I publicly surrendered to Jesus.

For a while, I held onto this idea that God was this magical creature. Someone who would instantly heal me just because I had accepted Him. I read, *come to me, all of you who are weary and carry heavy burdens, and I will give you rest*. Matthew 11:28 NLT. I clung to that promise. Every Sunday, I would go to the altar and accept Him repeatedly, wondering why it wasn't working. - Jesus, take this heavy burden. You are supposed to make me feel lighter. Take away my pain. Why aren't you taking it? Why am I still carrying all this weight?

In my search for healing, I turned to Christian books about sexual abuse. With each one, I ended up feeling hopeless. I could not relate to the authors. Their stories did not offer me enough. I wanted to know what really happened. Were they only abused once? How long did it take for God to heal them? Could He fix something as broken as me? What was the healing process like? I needed the details.

Even among Christians, the topic of sexual abuse seems like something to be ashamed of. Something to talk about in secret.

People tend to portray the gospel in the best conceivable way. As Christians, we want to share the beauty of following Christ, and in doing so, we avoid talking about the bad and the ugly. If I share the painful parts of my spiritual experience, how can I expect someone to want to know Jesus? So instead, people only tell the good of congregating, the miracles, and the transformation. They speak of becoming a new creation in Christ, and the idea is beautiful. I want to experience a magical transformation and receive a new purpose.

A person might testify, I was diagnosed with cancer, and God healed me. Talk about the bell at the end of the hallway. When celebrating the miracle, we tend to skip the pain, the weight of the illness. The prayers laced with anguish, the days when hope barely flickered. And the prayers from a broken heart with a trembling voice. Because the story of the bells sounds much better. Just as when it comes to sexual abuse, it is common to skip the journey. We do not discuss dirtiness or ashes. We focused on the new clothing and shoes that cover the marked body and wounded feet.

I found myself surrounded by a church community that welcomed me. Learning things that I should have known as a child. For the first time in my life, I felt like I belonged. Jesus became a whole new world. I fell in love with Jesus, and though I could not see him, he became my everything. The book I once was not allowed to read became a bond of love that kept pulling me in. Yet even in this newfound faith, I felt lonely. I was still walking in shackles.

I attend church every Sunday, filled with expectation of what God might do. I respect that the pastor always encourages us to read the Bible for ourselves. He often says, don't say amen just because I said it's in the Bible; go home and read it! But this Sunday, something he said stayed with me. He said, if you can find your problem in the Bible, then you are good, because when there's a problem, God always gives a solution. But if the Bible doesn't address your issue, then you have a problem.

The next morning, I found myself once again standing at the start line, ready to begin the journey towards healing. Before I took that first step onto the bumpy, uncertain road of recovery, I had a conversation from the depths of my heart with the Holy Spirit.

Holy Spirit, I've tried so many times to walk this road, and every time I've given up. I believe you can heal me. I believe you can break the chains that still limit my life. But I don't know how your healing works; it must be terrifying and painful, because no one ever wants to talk about it. Jesus said you would be with us until the end. Will you come with me now? Instead of me walking alone and getting lost again, will you guide me? Will you hold my hand and walk this path with me? If you want to heal me in the blink of an eye, I am here. But if healing takes time, if it means carefully gathering every broken piece of me, I understand. I know it won't be easy to look into the shattered mirror of my life. But I believe you can fix me. I'm willing to hold tightly to your hand and follow you. Please, don't give up on me, even if I give up on myself. Wait for me; I can't do this alone.

Do you want to get well? To read that question in the Bible and take it personally doesn't make sense, but the question echoes in my heart. Do you want to get well? I now understand that man who was lying by the Bethesda pool. When Jesus saw him and learned that he had been in that condition for a long time, He asked him, **Do you want to get well?** Sir, the man replied, I have no one to help me into the pool when the water is stirred. While I'm trying to get in, someone else goes down ahead of me. John 5:6–7, NIV

That is precisely how it feels when the Holy Spirit moves and everyone seems to receive something, and I remain unchanged. It's as if others dive into the wave of His presence, and just when I try, the wave crashes against the shore. The answer is yes. I want to get well. Now here is another question to face: Are you ready to get well?

There's nothing more painful than ripping a scab from a wound and having to restart the healing process. Sometimes, tearing it too early can cause the wound to go deeper. Many of us picked up that lesson early in life. The Band-Aid may have lost its glue, yet we still press it back in place. The scar will stay with us forever and is not pretty. The Holy Spirit is that doctor who isn't afraid to look closely. He wants to remove the temporary bandages I've used to hide the injury. He wishes to begin the process the right way. To examine the wound, cleanse it and then treat it properly until it heals.

In the agony of pain, we all long for that moment when healing breaks God's silence.

In Search of Healing

15

But I will restore you to health and heal your wounds,
declares the Lord. Because you are called an outcast,
Zion for whom no one cares.

Jeremiah 30:17

Some brethren in Christ seem to carry this expectation that God always heals instantly, almost as if there's a time limit on his power. You've been a Christian for how long, and you're still not free? It must be your lack of faith. Others claim it's simple; just forgive, and healing will follow. I fasted, read the Bible, and prayed, but still, my life was ruled by the post-traumatic echoes of my past. I was the opposite of what religion said I should be.

I thought the Holy Spirit would make this journey quick and easy, like He had a set of divine cheat codes to fast-forward the process. I was wrong. He wasn't rushing; healing is not a race to see who reaches the finish line faster. In my case it is the opposite; it is a walk. I realize that some people are only present at the beginning of the race, when it's easy to cheer you on. Others wait at the finish line, ready to celebrate, disappearing during the hardest part: the middle. That's when I felt most alone. No one really knew my story. I felt misunderstood and ashamed. I followed the directions people gave me, only to end up on dead-end roads. The ones who swore their path led to freedom had never walked it themselves.

Am I the only one on this road? If one in four women has been sexually abused, why is the church so silent? To my surprise, God wasn't silent. He knew it all and understood every step. He didn't place a deadline on my healing or wait for me at the finish line. Instead, He chose to walk beside me. He cheered me on when I was about to give up. He helped me up when I fell. While pain blurred my vision, he remained focused on the path. He was my guide, my rest, and my strength. When I ask, why is it taking so long? I can hear Him whisper, There's no hurry, one step at a time.

The Holy Spirit brought me to a path covered in thorns, with a single beautiful flower waiting at the end. It's painful to walk through. I'm not sure if I'll ever make it across. That's why I gave up so many times. I want to trust God. I want to be free. But I made my own terms and stayed stuck among the thorns. I know he could transform my life instantly, yet he chooses to start at the very beginning. Why? All I need to do is reach out to the flower, but every time I try, the thorns stab me. I might not succeed.

God was trying to become my father, and I couldn't let him. He would say, *I am your father,* and I would push back. Do not touch that part of my life. Every question I carried about my parents, every memory of rejection, became a thorn ready to pierce me. He is my God, my savior, my redeemer. I can call him all those names, just not Father. How can I see God as Father when the one I had hurt me so deeply? But over and over he says, I want to adopt you; I will call you my daughter, and you will call me father.

It sounds beautiful, a promise that feels as unreachable as the rose. There is so much pain and bitterness surrounding my parents. No one has ever loved me as a daughter. What kind of father is God? Will I become a hindrance to him? Does he see me as my mother?

When my father and my mother forsake me, then the Lord will take me up. —Psalm 27:10 (KJV)
He tends his flock like a shepherd: He gathers the lambs in his arms and carries them close to his heart. —Isaiah 40:11a (NIV)

He carried me out, just like a father lifting his little girl. He took me into his arms, adopted me, and held me close to his heart. He calls me daughter, and I call him Father.

After walking through the thorns, I thought the worst of my journey was over. Being able to rest in the green pastures at the feet of my adoptive father is priceless. He helps me overcome my fears and accept parts of myself I once hated. For example, I hated my name because my mother was the one who chose it. But lying in those pastures, I came to understand it was God who named me. One day, during a church service while I was worshiping, I had a vision: a sword engulfed in blue flames. It was unlike anything I had ever seen majestic and radiant. I couldn't help but wonder why I was seeing this sword. Then God spoke gently to my spirit: *I was the one who called you by name.* The name Brenda means sword.

But now, O Jacob, listen to the Lord who created you. O Israel, the one who formed you says, Do not be afraid, for I have ransomed you. I have called you by name; you are mine. —Isaiah 43:1 NLT

It was time to get back on the recovery road. There's still a long journey ahead, and we're only at the beginning. I feel invincible; I survived the thorns. My body bears the scratches. Leaving a few scars, thin and barely visible, each one tells a story. A memory of a moment when hope was missing. A second when a thorn pierced my arm, and I quietly wished for the end. A self-inflicted wound to cope. And even when the pain blinded me, He stayed.

With all my heart I will praise you, O Lord my God. I will give glory to your name forever, for your love for me is very great. You have rescued me from the depths of death. —Psalm 86:12-13 NLT

Church elders often say to cut the tree from the roots. So, it made sense to start with my parents' lack of love and abandonment. But that was just one root, and this tree had many.

I found myself walking down a dark path. The further I went, the darker it got. I had just been in the presence of my father, resting in the steadiness of his love, and now I was inside a cave of terror. I'm a born-again Christian trying to live a new life, yet here I am surrounded by depression and its gang. Feeling alone, it's so dark I can't see God. I feel sad, empty, and ashamed. I don't dare to ask for help, since depression is not supposed to control the life of a Christian. At least, that's what the stigma says. In church, it's often considered something shameful. Some use God's word like a magical wand.

Your word is a lamp for my feet, a light on my path. —Psalm 119:105 I quoted Scripture as if it would cast the darkness out on command. But it didn't work that way. The Holy Spirit was teaching me to trust Him, to believe in His Word, even when I couldn't see it working.

Instead of joy, the darkness came in like a thick cloud, smothering the path beneath my feet. What once felt like a spacious road turned into an unstable rope bridge that led me into a narrow, suffocating cave. Those butterflies the Christians love to talk about. They transformed into bats. And every time their wings flapped, they brought with them another flashback. Every second felt like my last. I was under constant attack from depression, anxiety, and panic. One thing about depression is it doesn't matter who's with you. You still feel alone. It's an enemy that invades the mind and heart, determined to take full control of your thoughts and emotions.

I asked so many times, why? But that question never seems to have an answer. The few people who know a little about my story say things like, now you'll be able to understand and help others. They tell me I have a testimony, or it made you stronger. But if it took so much suffering for me to understand and help other people, then, where is the person who is supposed to help me? After all, I'm not the first, and I won't be the last, just like my mother said. The torture I survived didn't make me stronger. I was already strong. I refuse to give my abusers the credit for my survival.

I didn't want to be stronger, or a superhero made of steel. I wanted to be a child. To fall off my bike, scrape my knees, and cry. To be disappointed because dessert came after dinner, not before breakfast. To scream at night about a monster in the closet and have a parent come to my rescue. The monsters in my closet were real.

Now, those memories are hitting me like a storm. I feel like a little girl who was left alone to face the monsters. I've been led into this dark cave, and I don't feel strong enough to confront them all. So, I sat in the corner and cry. Day after day. Night after night. Week after week. Month after month. Year after year. It's not a lack of faith. It's not about trust. There's no such thing as just grabbing your healing from the air. To act it out prophetically or lift your sword and march into freedom. There is no magic wand. The pain and terror are real. I'm not jumping in joy; I'm drowning in sorrow.

Bring me out of prison so I can thank you. The godly will crowd around me, for you are good to me. —Psalm 142:7 NLT

Inside the cave, I can hear the enemy telling me to put my head down and the voices of the past reminding me that I am worthless. My mind tortured me while searching for that moment when I smiled. The smile that was mistaken as an invitation. In the cave, my thoughts echo louder, with each tear falling like a raindrop. In there I collapse, hiding my face in shame.

We hear about these motivational speakers, but to a person who is battling depression, it can feel like false hope. It is like handing out basic first aid kits, hoping to reach the wounded. Forgetting that some wounds do not always heal instantly with a Band-Aid, they might require more intensive care.

I can't stand tall and walk freely while being terrorized by rabid bats. So, I begin to pray as I crawl. - Please, guide me with your voice, and I will follow you to freedom.

As I crawl deeper, the air grows heavier, the cave darker. It becomes scarier, and my tears grow thicker. Not knowing that the deeper I went, the closer I was to the exit. Until I made it across and saw the light, then I realized the Holy Spirit wasn't waiting for me on the other side; He had been crossing it with me all along.

You keep track of all my sorrows. You have collected all my tears in your bottle. You have recorded each one in your book. My enemies will retreat when I call to you for help. This I know: God is on my side! I praise God for what he has promised; yes, I praise the LORD for what he has promised. —Psalm 56:8-10 NLT

Even though the Bible is filled with uplifting promises meant to shine light into the darkness, I had to understand that I might not always feel different after reading just one verse. For some, crying is considered weakness; there's even a saying: "Men don't cry." Over time, tears almost become shameful.

There's a story in the Bible about a girl named Tamar. She begged, pleaded, and bargained. Still, she was raped and then despised.

"No, my brother!" she cried. "Don't be foolish! **Don't do this to me!** Such wicked things aren't done in Israel. **Where could I go in my shame?** And you would be called one of the greatest fools in Israel. Please, just speak to the king about it, and he will let you marry me." <u>But Amnon wouldn't listen to her, and since he was stronger than she was, he raped her.</u> Then suddenly Amnon's love turned to hate, and he hated her even more than he had loved her. "Get out of here!" he snarled at her. "No, no!" Tamar cried. Sending me away now is worse than what you've already done to me. But Amnon wouldn't listen to her. He shouted for his servant and demanded, "Throw this woman out, and lock the door behind her." So, the servant put her out and locked the door behind her. She was wearing a long, beautiful robe, as was the custom in those days for the king's virgin daughters. But now **Tamar tore her robe and put ashes on her head. And then, with her face in her hands, she went away crying**. —2 Samuel 13:12-19 (NLT)

Tearing her robe and placing ashes on her head was an expression of grief and mourning. Her way of saying, something inside of me has been shattered.

I've covered my face in shame more times than I can count, only to find myself in the cave. That lonely place where we carry a bag full of sorrow and cry bitterly. A place where some go to surrender, others to die, and a few to resurrect.

The cave is a very intriguing place. It's dark, yet you can still see your reflection. A place that, one way or another, forces you to drop your baggage. It makes you hunch, crawl, and walk along the edges. It's where you have to break through stone walls just to make it across. A place where defeat becomes real, fear blinds the way, and death seduces even the strongest. It's easy to surrender, to sit down and wait for God to come rescue you. Or worse, to simply accept the failure as final. But the cave can also make you appreciate the rays of light that uncover hidden treasures. It's a place that strips you of what's unnecessary, making space for wonders in return. It can straighten your back and teach you to walk in low and high places.

The cave also invites you to write stories on the walls. It's the place of victory, where trust becomes the guide. Where resurrection takes place. A hidden refuge to hear God's voice.

I've taken a few trips to the cave throughout the years. Especially during the summer months. It has almost become a summer destination. Once, as I was coming out, I heard the soft, loving voice of the Holy Spirit say, keep going, don't give up! I was nearly defeated, feeling hopeless far from soaring above the clouds. All I knew was that to keep going meant surviving one more day. I've been fighting for years, and still, He tells me to keep going. But for how long?

Will I ever have a testimony of restoration?

Jesus, take a look at me. This is me. I kept crying, and the words couldn't leave my mouth. This is me! I finished the conversation in my head. Jesus, are you looking at me? Can you please give me one reason why I should keep going and not give up? Look at me. What can you do with me? Look at me, I have nothing.

Like the little girl I once was, I cried myself to sleep and received an answer to my prayer. Jesus gave me a reason. A reason that gives me the strength to keep going. Guiding me out of the cave every time I find myself in there. When I woke up, I felt him near, waiting to finish the conversation we had started. In the dream, he showed me what he could make out of me. He gave me a purpose. A new desire started to grow after he planted a small seed in my heart. But I have a problem: the shackles are still on my feet.

I'm twenty-two years old, and I've been a born-again Christian for four years. According to the man-made clock, something must be wrong with me. A baby will walk by twelve months. A duckling learns how to fly in sixty days. So how long does it take for a Christian to be healed? Here I am, doubting if my life can truly be transformed, because I feel damaged beyond repair. Does God even want to cleanse and fix someone like me?

I go back and buy more Christian books of survivor stories. Stories of abuse told in a few pages, with plenty of Bible verses and a happy, spiritual ending.

So, I compare myself to those authors and wonder if I have no chance because my abuse wasn't a one-time thing; it was constant, relentless, and stretched over years. Why can't my healing be like theirs? Quick, easy, and magical. Holy Spirit, what am I doing wrong?

Jesus, you gave me a purpose. You offered me a future. I know you rescued me. You are a God who sets free, who heals and restores. My childhood was stolen; they took everything from me. Yet they couldn't take the one thing I held onto: the hope of finding you. I've been holding on to that idea for as long as I can remember. All I ever wanted was for you to take me back. You came to my rescue, and You found me. Now what? Can you please finish the work on me?

You intended to harm me, but God intended it for good to accomplish what is now being done, the saving of many lives. Genesis 50:20 NIV.

A Past in Ruins

16

Forget the former things; do not dwell on the past.
See, I am doing a new thing!
Now it springs up; do you not perceive it?
I am making a way in the wilderness
and streams in the wasteland.

Isaiah 43:18-19 NIV

There are moments when I can see myself sitting in a beautiful green pasture with Jesus right by my side. In front of us flows a crystal-clear river. We can talk for hours or simply sit in silence and enjoy the view. My life has been surrounded by chaos, so I don't need to jump up and down with joy. Peace and quiet is what I've longed for since I was a little girl. Sadly, that kind of peace only came from a dog. When I was punished and sent to the closet, the dog would sit right beside me. That's where I first learned how to change the scenery in my mind. A little imagination kept me sane; it helped me survive the torture, and it became my coping mechanism.

The beauty about Jesus is that he meets you exactly where you are. Here I am! I stand at the door and knock. If anyone hears my voice and opens the door, I will come in and eat with that person, and they with me. — Revelation 3:20 (NIV). A few of those times when he knocked, I was sitting in a corner—trying to gather my thoughts, still figuring out life, even as a Christian. But Jesus didn't mind where I was. He came in and sat with me on the floor. Without judgment or high expectations. I'm grateful he wasn't concerned about the state of my mind. I didn't have to pretend no one was home or ask him to wait while I swept things under the rug. I always opened the door because he never judged me.

I prayed to the Lord, and he answered me. He freed me from all my fears. Those who look to him for help will be radiant with joy; no shadow of shame will darken their faces. In my desperation, I prayed, and the Lord listened; he saved me from all my troubles. —Psalm 34:4-6 (NLT)

There's a story about a man who met Jesus at the lowest point of his life. He was literally chained and naked. What amazes me is that Jesus went looking for him. He covered the man's nakedness and allowed him to rest at his feet. Jesus didn't just free him; he also gave him a new purpose.

So they arrived in the region of the Gerasenes, across the lake from Galilee. As Jesus was climbing out of the boat, a man who was possessed by demons came out to meet him. For a long time, he had been **homeless** and **naked**, living in the tombs outside the town. —Luke 8:26–27 NLT. People rushed out to see what had happened. A crowd soon gathered around Jesus, and they saw the man who had been **freed** from the demons. He was **sitting at Jesus' feet, fully clothed** and perfectly sane, and they were all afraid. Then those who had seen what happened told the others how the demon-possessed man had been healed. —Luke 8:35–36 (NLT)

Stories like this give me hope. Jesus didn't hesitate to find that man. He didn't reject him because he wasn't wearing a suit and tie. He didn't stop to hear the rumors about his life. Jesus met him just as he was, and that's precisely what I need. So, every day, I open the door and meet Jesus just as I am, trusting that He will restore me.

—Jesus, I am desperate. I can't move beneath the weight of these shackles and chains. You are everything I seek. Thank you for meeting me just as I am. I trust you and your process in me. No matter how long it takes, I know you will set me free.

Brenda, write your story. I heard His loving voice so clearly. My story? I asked, hesitant and full of disbelief. Yes, write your story, he replied. Jesus, are you seeing me? What am I supposed to write about?

Write your story. You complain about others not providing details; write yours with details. You think they had a beautiful healing process just because they only shared the beauty of it. Write your story with the ugly side; write it just as it is. Write the book you've been searching for. The one that describes sorrow and pain, showing shame and guilt. Write your story, because even when you think you're the only one, you're not. You always ask if I see you, if I saw you. You wonder where I was, where I am. Write your story just as it is. Through the process, I will heal you. And you would discover for yourself if I witnessed it all, if I truly see you.

Writing my story sounds like a good idea. Something private that no one will read. I write a brief summary of my life, only to rip out the pages as soon as I finish. Getting rid of the evidence of my shame. At the same time, I was angry because I was still keeping the secret.

Jesus, here is my story. I still can't see you. How can a loving God disregard my pain? You want me to write my story? Who will read it? Who would want to read a book like this? It's impossible to believe that you saw what happened and did nothing. You could have rescued me. Why didn't you come sooner? Why didn't you take me back or let me die? You took too long. Where were you when I needed you most? Why do you allow bad things to happen? If I write my story, how can I give you glory? It will be a book full of pain, and no God in sight. A book full of thorns and no roses.

While ripping the pages, I can hear his voice insisting for me to write my story, and I do it over and over again. As I begin to see all the violence and injustice done to me. I realized I have no one to console me. I was raised in silence, in a place both blind and deaf. Waiting for a God who didn't show up.

As a child, I met an impostor dressed in religious clothing who never cared to cover anyone's nakedness. I met entertainers who played instruments but didn't know how to worship. Preachers who spoke the word of God but never took a moment to listen to Him. I found myself in places where no one valued me. A few coins, a paper bag, alcohol, diapers, and pills were all on display. A kiss, a touch, a movie, mocking, a slap, and stabbing words. That's what I received.

So many messages were sent to God, tied to balloons from the garden of thorns. Pending messages, unanswered, lost in pain. Still, I trust him and continue to write my story.

I walked a journey without knowing my destination, shattered and lost. I've longed for death because even the idea of hell didn't feel as terrifying as my reality. Terror became my legal guardian and tortured me. Gifting me a box full of punishments, wrapped in shame and guilt. What started as a wishful dream turned into a nightmare. Where crying myself to sleep was no longer an option, and running into the sky became exhausting. I longed for a safe castle while suffocating in a closet. Quietly waiting on a God who seemed too busy to care. Still, I trust him and continue to write my story.

I turned off the strong woman and became once again the little girl, carrying the heavy burden of dirty secrets. Trying to show the chains and the shackles on my feet. Willing to expose my nakedness, lifting my head even when I feel ashamed. I don't know how to raise my trembling voice, or if anyone will hear me. Yet I long to become a maul in hopes to break the silence. With a broken heart and tears in my eyes. Still, I trust him and continue to write my story.

Shame always finds a way back in, and guilt is never far behind. How can you write about your childhood? Now your family will know your side of the story. Are you really going to give them details to spread around? No one will believe you. You can't call yourself a victim. You had sex with your brother-in-law because you didn't want him with another of your sisters. Isn't that jealousy? Did you really write about the box? You're as guilty as they are. A book with no happy ending? Where was God in all of this? Why does He allow bad things to happen? Is God even real, or an imaginary friend?

I feel damaged and worthless. I've heard so many negative words all my life; they've become engraved in me. Like a broken record echoing in my mind. I internalized the blame, convinced I was responsible. I should've screamed louder. I should've asked clearly for help. I wasn't strong. I deserved it. Every thought made me feel ashamed. Therefore, I can't tell anyone my side of the story. I am the one to blame. I got what I deserved.

And when something is shameful, instinct says it must be hidden. So, I hide myself, straight into isolation.

Shame is painful. It makes me feel exposed and vulnerable. But I chose to open up, and as I did, I began laying my burdens on the table. I uncovered my deepest wounds, my pain, and my sorrow. I opened the door and let Jesus in. Over and over, until I could trust him with all the dirty secrets I'd been carrying. It might seem as if it doesn't make sense. Why do I need to trust him or tell him my life when He knows it all? Perhaps I am writing my story for me. Maybe it is me who needs to see and hear the version of the little girl who was neglected and abused. To silence the perpetrator's voice, I must hear my version. I must write my story and allow the voice of my inner child to be heard. After all, she wanted to write a book.

I opened up to him like a book as I wrote my story. And in doing so, I realized there's nothing good about me. Nothing beautiful to be proud of. The joy of his promises began to fade in the face of shame. I got stuck going back and forth between faith and shame. Guilt and forgiveness, abandonment and hope.

I made it out of the garden of thorns and survived the cave. Only to find myself lost in the desert. I faced the pain of the thorns and endured the terror of the cave. Now I must face the scorching sun, the drought, and the instability of shifting sand. Wondering once again if I will be able to survive. If Jesus will be walking by my side or if I will perish. What does the desert hold for me? Will He be able to find me if I get lost in my pain?

I can stare at a painting of the desert and be amazed by it. Admire the color palette shaped by earthy tones, awed by how these tiny grains of sand build a world of their own. They cover the ground with soft waves, shifting gently as the wind carries them. Portraits tend to show the beauty of the scene, just as we tend to talk about the sunrise and sunset but not the sunburn. Finding myself in a desert, it's nothing like those pictures. I do not belong to a group of tourists on a trip.

It's a landscape of sand with terrain that threatens my footing, filled with obstacles that test my stability. I am struggling to stand firm. The horizon stretches out like my future: it seems distant and unreachable. Feeling like a single grain of sand that disappears in this vast, isolated place. Loneliness convinces me to stay silent, to keep my voice locked inside. Even if I tried to speak, there's no one to hear me. There's only the whistling wind cutting through the silence.

Alone in this desert, I catch a glimpse of a mirage, God's promises shimmering in the distance. An optical illusion of what he could do with me. But the oasis keeps slipping farther away with every step I take, and hope evaporates like boiling water. At some point, the heat of the circumstances and the exhaustion from running catch up. I'm stuck, with no water and no strength. I would love to run away, but I don't know which direction to take. I practically just got here, and I am already feeling lost. There's no tour, no map, or directions. Just me wanting to run away from the reality of my past. Trying to escape in the hope of finding a new version of myself.

Did I run into the desert to escape, or did God bring me here?

Here is where I meet with my true self. A hidden place where I can remove the armor and expose my deepest wounds. The perfect place to protest and scream. A place to cry my heart out. Where no one sees me, no one hears me, and I can finally bury my shame and guilt.

Just like the people of Israel, I too complained and questioned God.

Moses, we'd be better off if we had died along with the others in front of the Lord's sacred tent. You brought us into this desert, and now we and our livestock are going to die! Egypt was better than this horrible place. —Numbers 20:3-5a CEV

What's the purpose of keeping me alive? How can a loving God allow such things?

I learned how to survive slavery. I knew what was expected of me, and I had lost hope. Now here I am, trying to know a God who offers freedom and restoration. I attend a church where people seem happy, walking in freedom, as if God Himself empowered them. So why can't I experience freedom as a whole?

It feels like Pharaoh's army is right behind me, about to catch me. Waiting for the moment I turned around. As if they know how hard this battle will be for me to win. Everyone seems to have a weapon, and I have none. How can I be set free from my enemies? I feel like a dog chained to a fence; no matter how hard I try to run, it always pulls me back to them. I end up going back to the bowl of water.

I heard that forgiveness is essential to being free. So, I must forgive those who hurt me. What? That's really in the Bible?

Bear with each other and forgive one another if any of you has a grievance against someone. Forgive as the Lord forgave you. — Colossians 3:13 (NIV)

The idea of forgiving those who hurt me really bothers me. I simply cannot comprehend why God would ask such a thing. When people discuss forgiveness, I wonder if it was actually as easy as they portray it to be. Did they ever stop to question it or even doubt for a moment? Can someone keep it real? Months have passed, and I'm still battling with my feelings. A part of me wants to give up. I don't think I'll ever be able to forgive. I'm not coming out of this place.

How can I adapt when death surrounds me? I see vultures circling above as I grow weaker. Once again, the oasis with the presence of God feels far away. A mirage that fades with time, as the hourglass runs out. I'm even considering turning away from Jesus. After all, it's easier to create a desert than to grow a forest. I feel desperate, stationed in a very dry place. I would give anything to satisfy this thirst. I need Jesus to help, but he's been silent.

I've been in this drought for a long time. Out of desperation, I begin to whisper a prayer. I forgive X. I forgive X. I speak the names of fourteen men and two women. Then I add, and those whose names I don't know.

My longing for God's presence turns into a flood of emotions as I speak their names. The sand beneath my feet shifts and softens, threatening to swallow me. It's like sinking in quicksand. Every single name suffocates me. Just to think that my freedom depends on forgiving them makes me feel like my freedom is in their hands. Are they still controlling me? That thought alone makes it feel like my bones are being crushed. The pain is too much to bear. My lips stay sealed, unwilling to ask for help. How can I explain that even though I'm naming them, I still can't forgive them?

So, keeping it real. That is how months turned into years. It wasn't lack of faith, but because the wounds were too deep and a Band-Aid wasn't enough.

Time is an expert in leaving things behind, just as sand is an expert in covering evidence. Together, they make a deadly team. The stories of countless victims lie buried in the desert. They are still there, unseen, unheard of unless someone dares to dig them out.

Jesus… they don't deserve forgiveness. You don't understand me. No one does. As I whisper those words, tears blur my vision. For I fear I will never be set free. How can I forgive them? The storm may have passed but look at all the havoc it left behind. They took so much from me, things I'll never get back. Who can I relate to? I can still smell his sweat and taste his saliva. Feel the burn from the cigarettes. See my father's eyes, taste the alcohol on his breath. I hear the mockery. I wake up suffocating, gasping for air, trying to fight off the invisible hands around my neck.

I would rather not be a victim. But how can I call myself a survivor when my past became a shadow that follows me in the present? Make a survivor out of me. Help me come out of this place. How can you be silent? Where are you? Do you even care?

Suddenly, the mirage changes. Jesus shifts the scene, and now I see the reflection of the cross. As I look at it, my soul finds comfort. Not by peeking into my future, but by gazing into Jesus past. As I study his life on earth, I realize I cannot fully relate to him, but he truly understands me. He felt discomfort, laying his head on a rock. He gave everything to others, even went looking for them, only to be left alone. He was betrayed, sold, mocked, beaten, and spat on. They stripped him of his clothes, and his nakedness was exposed. He was humiliated. He knows what it's like to be tired and thirsty, to carry someone else's burden. He was rejected. And on that cross, he endured the sting of abandonment, the heartbreaking silence from a parent. He knows fear and what it feels like to scream with a trembling voice. He, like me, knows that the only way out is to look at the sky in hopes for God to rescue you. He also heard God's silence.

Unlike me, he chose all that suffering. Willingly put himself in that position. He believes we are worth saving. I survived while he died. He volunteered to pay the highest price for you and me. And even then, one of his final words was, Father, **forgive them, for they don't know what they are doing.** —Luke 23:34a NLT

He Found Me

17

Then you will call on me and come and pray to me,
and I will listen to you. You will seek me
and find me when you seek me with all your heart.
I will be found by you, declares the LORD,
and will bring you back from captivity.

Jeremiah 29:12-14a NLT

Suddenly, I had this thought that it was easier for Jesus to forgive. For a moment, I lost sight of his humanity and imagined him as a God made of steel and stone, immune to pain, far from my suffering. How could he possibly understand me?

Though he was God, he did not think of equality with God as something to cling to. Instead, he gave up his divine privileges; he took the humble position of a slave and was born as a human being. When he appeared in human form, he humbled himself in obedience to God and died a criminal's death on a cross. Philippians 2:6–8 NLT.

My limited mind wrestles with this. People say forgiveness is for my own good, but pain has blinded me. While I lie awake in the middle of the night, they sleep soundly. While I walk in fear, glancing over my shoulder, they move confidently. Hunting for their next prey. Forgiveness isn't as simple as people make it sound. It's deeper than a whispered prayer or a name spoken aloud.

Jesus said, You have heard the law that says, 'Love your neighbor' and hate your enemy. But I say, love your enemies! Pray for those who persecute you! — Matthew 5:43–44 NLT

I've been stuck in the desert so long that months turned into years. It feels like my roots have grown above the surface. I've become hardened, like a cactus weathering every storm. But I don't want this to be my legacy. To pass down the thorns to the generations after me. I refuse to let my pain become my family tree. I need to cut these roots; I can't stay bound to these chains.

I frequently questioned myself, especially in the silence that followed my prayers. One prayer didn't seem to be enough. The doubts came like insect bites. Small, sharp attacks that I didn't notice until after being stung. Still, I kept walking, determined to reach the Oasis. Crawling many times, convinced it was all in vain. While deep down inside, I was still searching for that one person who understood me. Someone to give me hope, proof that this isn't the end of me. I need to know that this is not the end of my story.

There may never be an answer to all my questions. Maybe I'll never understand why. But one thing is clear to me: if I don't keep moving forward, I will die. I'm not strong enough to do this alone, but I've come too far to turn back now. I'm nearing the finish line. If I don't finish, there are only two outcomes: I'll have to start over, to revisit the Garden of Thorns, the Dark Cave, and the Desert. Or I'll be disqualified, therefore forced to sit beside my family in silence and watch someone else take the place that was meant for me.

I must finish my journey.

I stepped into this desert believing the Holy Spirit would walk with me. Just as he did through the Garden of Thorns and the Cave. And I know that, like before, he'll be here at the darkest point, offering refuge. It was in his presence that I saw the most beautiful flower blooming in the garden and the rays of light dancing between the crystal rocks in the cave. The darkness of the desert will not dull the stars. And even when thirst threatens to kill me, I believe there will be a hidden well in this wilderness. Jesus will find me.

No little girl dreams of becoming a young maid to a wicked master. They all pretend to be princesses, imagining castles and stories with happy endings. Just like girls play the roles of princesses, Christian women often identify with women in the Bible. I once attended a women's Bible study where the question was asked, who do you relate to in the Bible? Sarah seems to be popular. Reading the story of Sarah, I found myself in the margins, inside the life of a slave. Her name was Hagar, a young slave.

Hagar was a gift from a king to Sarai. She became the concubine, the maid, the slave. Sarah's story is popular, her heartbreak over infertility and her desperation to fulfill God's promise. But few stop to see the pain Sarah caused in her efforts to fix it. She turned her eyes toward the young girl who had no voice, no choice, and no rights, only orders to obey.

Now Sarai, Abram's wife, had not been able to bear children for him. But she had an Egyptian servant named Hagar. So Sarai said to Abram, "The Lord has prevented me from having children. **Go and sleep with my servant.** Perhaps I can have children through her." And Abram agreed with Sarai's proposal. So Sarai, Abram's wife, **took Hagar, the Egyptian servant, and gave her to Abram as a wife. Abram had sexual relations with Hagar**, and she became pregnant. But when Hagar knew she was pregnant, she began to treat her mistress, Sarai, with contempt. Then Sarai said to Abram, "This is all your fault! I put my servant into your arms, but now that she's pregnant, she treats me with contempt. The Lord will show who's wrong, you or me!" Abram replied, "Look, she is your servant, so deal with her as you see fit." Then Sarai treated Hagar so harshly that she finally ran away. Genesis 16:1–6 NLT

I finally found my problem in the Bible. With the lack of information in the story of my birth, there's no love nor joy. I was this little girl whose feelings didn't matter because my destiny was to remain silent and obedient. My opinion was irrelevant; my voice was not heard. I played different roles; I entertained my brother, ran errands for my mother, and became her in front of my father. With every order that I obeyed, the volume of my voice was lowered until I became silent, mute just like my mom. I was passed onto my sister's hand; she welcomed me into her house not as a family member but as a slave. Determined to keep her partner by her side, she obtained me as a mere object. Even though it was with other intentions and other circumstances, my sister repeated the words of Sara: Go and sleep with my slave.

"Brenda is crying because she wants to have sex." "Brenda is happy because she desires to have sex." Just like Hagar, I had no choice but to obey. It is because of God's mercy that I didn't become pregnant. He shielded me; I don't know if I was strong enough to bear his child. To witness them killing and giving the blood of a little boy to the Indian, or to witness her claiming to be the mother of a little girl.

I should be feeling relieved for finding my problem in the Bible; it means that there is also a solution for me. Or even better, the story of Hagar means that Jesus is about to meet me, and his silence is about to be broken. I'm coming out from the desert and soon will be crossing the finish line of my journey. But far from feeling hopeful, I feel heartbroken.

Everyone wants to be Sara, whose name, by the way, means princess. Everyone dreams of being the chosen one, the beloved, the bearer of a promise. But no one wants to be Hagar, or forsaken, as her name implies. We talked about how Sara's plan was a mistake and how Hagar became a complication, she and her child both. We draw spiritual lessons from it: as we should wait on God's timing, we shouldn't take matters into our hands. Some even say this was normal for the time, as if that makes it acceptable. Rarely do we talk about the feelings of this young slave. Assuming she had none, just as she had no choice. Over and over, her story is overlooked like she was.

The angel of the Lord found Hagar near a spring in the desert; it was the spring beside the road to Shur. And he said, Hagar, slave of Sarai, **where have you come from, and where are you going**? I'm running away from my mistress, Sarai, she answered. —Genesis 16:7–8 NIV

Once again, he comes and finds someone in need, right where she is. He already knows where she's been and where she's going; still, He asks. Because he wants her to have a voice. When Jesus comes to meet us, he gives us space to tell our story. He wants us to know him just as he already knows us. We matter to him. He wants us to *see* the One who *sees* us.

She gave this name to the Lord who spoke to her: "You are the God who sees me," for she said, "I have now seen the One who sees me." —Genesis 16:13 (NIV)

God's word became like water in the desert, an oasis full of his presence. And for once, it didn't disappear like a mirage.

Hagar's story didn't end when she met the one who saw her. After her encounter with God, she returned to Sarai. She gave birth to a son, and for a while, they lived under the same roof. Eventually, she became a hindrance again. An unwanted reminder of a plan gone wrong. This time, Sarai told Abraham to get rid of her.

Abraham got up early the next morning, prepared food and a container of water, and strapped them on Hagar's shoulders. Then he sent her away with their son, and she wandered aimlessly in the wilderness of Beersheba. When the water was gone, she put the boy in the shade of a bush. Then she went and sat down by herself about a hundred yards away. "I don't want to watch the boy die," she said as she burst into tears. —Genesis 21:14–16 NLT

Like Hagar, I've found myself wandering in the desert more than once. Walking without direction, no plan, no purpose. Life often sends me away without enough water to survive. In that kind of dryness, we learn to adapt. In the middle of the desert, you don't reject a sip of water just because it's rainwater and not from a clean, name-brand bottle. You drink it, even if you have to share the puddle with an animal. Just like I shared with a dog in a closet. I adapted until they decided I was no longer needed. I was getting too old and became a threat. My sister feared I'd take her "wife" title.

In the desert, a child in your arms becomes everything: hope, family, dreams, and future. But when there's no more escape, when your strength runs out, and your hope dries up. All you can do is fall apart, burst into tears, and surrender.

There's a difference between cries. When you still have strength left to wipe your tears and keep pushing forward. Fighting to survive, trying over again today and tomorrow. To cry when you've given it all, when there's nothing left: no strength, no hope. That cry is the cry of surrender, knowing it might mean the end of you. To lay down your future, to turn away only to face death. It is brokenness on another level. It is the heartbreak of being condemned, swallowed by overwhelming, perpetual self-pity.

God heard the boy crying, and the angel of God called to Hagar from heaven and said to her, **"What is the matter, Hagar?** Do not be afraid; God has heard the boy crying as he lies there. Lift the boy up and take him by the hand, for I will make him into a great nation." Then God opened her eyes, and she saw a well of water. So, she went and filled the skin with water and gave the boy a drink. —Genesis 21:17–19 NIV

God cannot resist a broken heart. I imagine God hearing this cry and stopping everything, just like we do when a newborn cries in the house. We pause, we pay close attention, and rush to meet the baby's needs. God does the same when a broken heart surrenders.

He already knows your problem, where you've come from, and where you are going. He knows what the matter is. Still, He wants to hear your voice. He wants you to tell your story.

The Lord hears his people when they call to him for help. He rescues them from all their troubles. The Lord is close to the brokenhearted; he rescues those whose spirits are crushed. —Psalm 34:17-18 NL

As Jesus meets me where I am, suddenly my problems feel small. Brenda, what's the matter? A few seconds earlier, I had given up, still clinging to a list of unanswered questions. However, they were no longer significant. So instead of asking why, I simply handed Him my broken heart. At times we have no words. We don't know where we're coming from or where we're going. Still, Jesus finds us. He listens and gives me space to cry. I didn't have to speak; still, He heard me. I didn't have to show Him where it hurt; He saw me. He wiped the tears from my eyes and healed my wounds. He clothed me and covered up my nakedness.

In the oasis, I came to understand a few things. I had believed I would never forgive, because praying for some people made me feel enraged. I didn't realize that God feels the same anger toward those who deliberately harm others, especially children.

The Lord examines the righteous, but the wicked, those who love violence, He hates with a passion. —Psalm 11:5 NIV

But if you cause one of these little ones who trust in me to fall into sin, it would be better for you to be thrown into the sea with a large millstone hung around your neck. —Mark 9:42 NLT

As I laid my burdens before Jesus, I saw His justice more clearly. He is a fair God. I no longer needed revenge, for I could trust his judgment. At times I feel victorious every time I speak about my past. My voice was what they feared the most. Jesus knew this, so he removed the seal from my lips. When He asked me to write my story, it wasn't just a way to process my pain; it was to form a weapon against those who love violence.

Now I can see that every time I hid under the bed, Jesus was right by my side. His presence was stronger than my fear. I see him now, pulling me back when I tried to take my life. I saw Him in the water, reaching for me as I was drowning. He was with me on the plane, responding to my message, telling me, **it will be okay.**

Jesus showed me the clear sky, allowing me to run free while searching for a castle. When the enemy surrounded me, he became my shield. When my mind unraveled in the closet, he sat right beside me.

They touched my body and crushed my spirit. They broke my heart and did evil things to me. But they couldn't take away my faith. Even when they portrayed Him as a punisher, and I felt abandoned, I still believed he would save me. And he did; Jesus found me!

I still don't understand why me. I became the victim of victims who had become perpetrators themselves. I was the easy prey, surrounded by the wounded who were left behind. I must be the family member who stepped in for the one who couldn't finish the journey before me. The next in line to face the enemy in a long war for freedom. Maybe I was just the daughter of a slave, born into slavery. We all face different battles, so the reasons for me, might not make sense in your story. That's okay. I'm not trying to answer your questions.

But I do know that it is ok to ask God why He allows bad things to happen. It's ok to wonder where God was. Jesus won't turn away from your questions or your pain. You don't need to hide when He calls. He already knows where you're coming from. Still, He's looking for you. It's okay not to be okay when he finds you.

Unlike many other survivors who encounter God and experience instant breakthroughs, my healing has been slow and long. I needed time to understand that my past is part of who I am, and even though Jesus healed me, that doesn't mean the memories got erased. It still hurts, deeper than expected. It took me years to write my story and share it. The abuse was real, and so is the pain it causes to remember. Occasionally I have to allow myself space to grieve for the little girl who was neglected and abused.

Like others, I give thanks to Jesus, because I know he is the one who made me a survivor. He knew I was waiting for him. He saw I was searching. So, He did what I couldn't do; *He found me.*

But I came by and saw you there, helplessly kicking about in your own blood. As you lay there, I said, 'Live!' And I helped you to thrive like a plant in the field. You grew up and became a beautiful jewel. Your breasts became full, and your body hair grew, but you were still naked. And when I passed by again, I saw that you were old enough for love. So, I wrapped my cloak around you to cover your nakedness and declared my marriage vows. I made a covenant with you, says the Sovereign Lord, and you became mine. Then I bathed you and washed off your blood, and I rubbed fragrant oils into your skin. I gave you expensive clothing of fine linen and silk, beautifully embroidered, and sandals made of fine goatskin leather. I gave you lovely jewelry, bracelets, beautiful necklaces, a ring for your nose, earrings for your ears, and a lovely crown for your head. And you were adorned with gold and silver. Your clothes were made of fine linen and costly fabric and were beautifully embroidered. You ate the finest foods, choice flour, honey, and olive oil and became more beautiful than ever. You looked like a queen, and so you were! - Ezekiel 16:6-13 NLT

This is my story, the one recorded through the eyes of a little girl. The one no one cared to see, while others turned a blind eye. A story many ignored as it was being lived and filmed in real time. This is my story: a faded reflection of countless others who were once where I stood. A story that reveals the monster who doesn't hide in the shadows.

This is my voice, the voice a little girl once tried to raise. The one that didn't always get heard, because silence can speak louder. A voice so many overlooked while it cried out in the dark. This is my voice: an echo of countless innocent victims who tried to speak, only to be silenced by abusers who blend into society and erase their victims in plain sight.

This is my story, the past that chased me down. The truth that no one wanted to see. My version, the one I lived and survived. This is my voice, the one that was once silenced and now refuses to stay quiet. A story being unearthed from the ruins. A journey toward freedom, healing, and restoration.

This is me, just as I am, breaking the silence. For me, for my family, and for the generations to come. Today, I can speak and be heard because there is a God who cared enough to save me.

The enemy told me to be quiet, but Jesus asked me to raise my voice louder. I decided to put aside the shame and follow the one who gave me a purpose when *He Found Me*.